PRAISE FOR U𝘕

"In *Unipreneur: How to Live Your Passion in a House Full of Dream-Killers*, Laura shares snippets of her journey toward a joyful, expansive, fruitful life even though her biggest obstacles often resided under the same roof. She writes as if the reader is sitting in the same room, having a heart-to-heart conversation, sharing both laughter and tears. Through the author's personal insights, practical methods, and eternal truths, readers have a golden opportunity to step upward to a life they absolutely love living."

—Mary Manin Morrissey, Life Coach,
Motivational Speaker, Best-selling Author,
Founder of Life Mastery Institute

"Take some time to read this inspiring book. Laura has done a great job of blending faith with practical business and life advice. Beautiful!"

—Glenn & Pam Shoffler, Multi-business Entrepreneurs,
Shoffler International, Inc.

"Everything is energy. The positive energy emanating from *Unipreneur: How to Live Your Passion in a House Full of Dream-Killers* can help open-hearted readers move forward with their dreams while, at the same time, developing deep, reciprocal relationships with loved ones that don't share their vision. Having personally witnessed the author forge forward on this enlightened path, I know that readers can learn from Laura's personal experiences and practical methods she shares. Read, apply, and live an abundant life!"

—Kirsten Welles, Master Coach,
LifeSOULutions That Work, LLC

"*Unipreneur* will show you a step-by-step how-to guide to building your self-esteem and your business. Laura will teach you to become a successful Unipreneur and show you how you can become successful even if you have to do it alone. This book is a quick and easy read. Enjoy!"

—**Omar Periu,** Best-selling Author, Speaker, Coach, Self-made Multi-millionaire, Omar Periu International

"Are you seeing a bigger story for your life? Are you bewildered about how to make it happen? While reading *Unipreneur,* you will go on one woman's journey to support planting your 'dream seeds' of opportunity. Through use of Laws of Success and Creation of a Vision, Laura takes us on her journey of spiraling up to being a woman whose life makes a bigger difference. What is your bigger story? Go ahead. Do it. Read *Unipreneur.* Listen to your inner wisdom rather than listening to the 'dream-killers' in your life. Step into your bigger story!"

—**Carolyn Rose Hart,** Award-winning Author, Speaker, Trainer, Coach, Founder and President of Step Up Step Out

"It's tough when you have a burning passion, but your loved ones don't share the same vision. Too often, people either give up on their dreams or give up the naysayers living under the same roof. In *Unipreneur: How to Live Your Passion in a House Full of Dream-Killers,* author Laura S. Shortridge shows how you can have both."

—**Kary Oberbrunner,** Author of *ELIXIR Project, Day Job to Dream Job, The Deeper Path,* and *Your Secret Name*

"I am so impressed with Laura Shortridge and *Unipreneur*. Laura's success as a businesswoman, real estate investor, and word weaver shines through in her book. With wit and wisdom, Laura walks readers through her personal journey, and teaches them how to shield and nourish their dream seeds. It feels like sitting down with a smart and funny friend who's sharing her best life, relationship, and business advice. It's honest, refreshing and inspiring! I'd highly recommend *Unipreneur* to anyone who has dreams to pursue. Laura's advice shows you how to protect your dream seeds and grow them into a bountiful garden!"

—Jane VanVooren Rogers, Freelance Editor, Author of *How to Avoid Being and Other Paths to Triumph*

UNIPRENEUR

*How to Live Your Passion
in a House Full of Dream-Killers*

LAURA S. SHORTRIDGE

Printed in the United States of America

Published by Author Academy Elite
P.O. Box 43, Powell, OH 43035

www.AuthorAcademyElite.com

Paperback: 978-1-64085-091-0

Hardback: 978-1-64085-092-7

Library of Congress Control Number: 2017950205

This book is dedicated to four dear friends who gave me loving support at crucial times on this journey: Justine Rylander, Betty Hales, Cheryl Downer, and Janet Smiley. They are among my "forever" friends.

CONTENTS

PREFACE

"You have to be burning with an idea or a problem,
or a wrong that you want to right.
If you're not passionate enough from the start,
you'll never stick it out."

—Steve Jobs

I truly believe that every individual on the planet has a divine connection with someone, something far greater than we can imagine. Personally, I believe in God, and in this book, I'll reference "Him" rather than Her or It. You are an infinite being having an earthly experience. You weren't created to live in a vacuum. Humans were meant to learn and grow through experience and choice. We were also meant to connect with and serve others.

When you have a brilliant idea and your heart burns with passion to pursue it, you've been given a divine gift to develop and share. Sometimes you have to do it alone, at least at first. I encourage you to move forward with your dreams even if just one baby step at a time. I echo the words attributed to Winston Churchill, "Never, never, never give up!"

As you read, I suggest you take notes. Lots and lots of notes! It will help speed up your journey.

I sincerely hope you'll read this more than once or at least refer back to underscored sections with which you resonate. I wish you all the best in your amazing journey!

INTRODUCTION

MY PATH TO BECOMING
A UNIPRENEUR

*"You can ask others for direction
about your life's path …
But remember, then you're on someone
else's journey and may get lost.
Search for your own path within."*

—Nanette Mathews

Have you ever had an idea pop into your head that sent shivers of excitement down your spine? Thoughts of it even now bring a grin to your face and a burning to your soul?

I'm not talking about negative things like ways to take revenge on that guy who sideswiped your car, or cons to swindle a grandma out of her life savings. Those ideas are dark and contractive.

I'm talking about a bona fide boon to impact you and your world in an expansive way. Something with powerful positive outcomes.

I call them dream seeds.

We all have them. The question is, what do you do with those tiny grains of creativity? Especially if you live with dream-killers that will stomp those little sprouts just as they break the surface. Me? I have lived in both worlds … a happy garden with flowers, sunshine, and a Fairy Godmother (okay, maybe not a Fairy Godmother) and a barren space with stones, darkness, and muddy bootprints.

My journey to becoming a unipreneur was painfully slow. It took over a decade to have any measure of success. Why? I had no one to direct me. Trial and error. Hit and miss. Clichés, I know, but that pretty well describes my stumblings. I will share an abbreviated account of those experiences, giving you a peek into my head and, therefore, my perspective.

After that, I'll share strategies and tools to live your passion in a house full of dream-killers. Part I will help you prepare yourself for unipreneurship, to help you be strong enough to overcome the blows of the naysayers. Part II will give insight into the minds of the dream-killers, which, in turn, will help you present your passion in an empowered way. Part III will give strategies to actively pursue your dreams while keeping good relationships with those dream-killers that you still love and want to keep in your life. Each chapter includes Action Steps for both pursuing your passion and strengthening your relationships. If you sincerely want positive change in your life, I suggest you follow through with them.

In the Beginning

I was a kid with lots of ideas. Fortunately, I lived in a nurturing environment with parents who let me plant my dream seeds. In fact, they encouraged it. My family members loved and supported me whether I had success or not. Well, except for one brother who wanted to slap postage on my forehead and mail me to China, but hey, we won't go there.

Around age 10, I decided I wanted to be a news reporter. I recruited a girl across the street to be my sidekick and we went around the neighborhood interviewing people for "The Crestwood Circle News." I intended this newsletter to be a weekly occurrence for my extended future. However, it took a full week just to catch someone from each household on our cul-de-sac.

The project took place in prehistoric times, way before computers or even copy machines. My mom had a home version of what was called a ditto machine. She let me use her typewriter to construct a three-page document on ditto master sheets. It contained glorious stories of birthday parties, vacation plans, visiting relatives ... Oh, and a missing cat.

It was a painstaking experience. I'm sure my angel mother helped me a lot more than I realized. I do remember that Mom had to run the ditto machine, and that the paper smelled funny when it came out. And the print was purple. It wasn't like the ditto machine at school on which the teachers pumped out dozens of copies. Our home version only copied around 10 pages before it got so faded it was unreadable. Then the same tedious process had to repeated for Page 2. Then Page 3.

So, I had 10 copies of a three-page newsletter, from dark purple words to very faint lavender ones. I kept a copy for myself, gave one to my sidekick, and sold the rest to amused neighbors for a quarter each. I'm sure my mother was giddy with relief when I decided one newsletter was enough to satisfy me.

My dream seed had been planted, nurtured, and then took a life of its own after it sprouted. It was not stomped out. Even though I no longer desired to be a news reporter, the dream of using written language to express and expand myself has continued to flourish even after 40+ years. Today I am a full-fledged word weaver.

There was a time, however, when my passion for writing (among some other dream seeds) was stuck way back on a shelf. Thank goodness, it was near an open window where a few sunbeams and an occasional raindrop would help it survive the distracted years. There was also a decade that I call my dark ages. More on that later.

Do you have dream seeds stuck in your head? Or stashed on a shelf somewhere? If you do, you aren't alone.

Planting Dream Seeds

In high school, we were given an assignment to write down dreams for our future. Besides becoming a philanthropy-minded writer and artist, I wrote down my main goals as becoming a wife and mother of six children. Whoa. Not sure where I came up with the number of children but after the assignment was returned to us, I promptly forgot about it. However, the dream seeds had been planted. In 2015, my essay resurfaced and, holy cow, it was an eye-opener to reread.

I got married at age 19 to my 23-year-old Prince Charming whom I met at college. We got engaged 11 days after our first date and tied the knot 4 months later. We had very different backgrounds and looking back, we really didn't know each other very well (duh ... who can after less than 6 months?).

But we had one very important connection that I thought would overcome any differences – and it did for about 18 years – our mutual belief in the Gospel of Jesus Christ. Our shared dream was to raise a righteous family, strong in the nurture and admonition of the Lord. Our commitment to God, our desire to follow Jesus Christ, our love for each other, we could go nowhere but up, right?

And guess what? We had six children. Just like I had written down in my high school essay. I was blessed with a husband, three sons, and three daughters (born in that order). I willingly put my other personal dreams on hold to give my full attention, effort, and love to my growing family. My desire to write was fulfilled by way of journaling my experiences. Every once in a while, I would get a short story or magazine article published, but writing was a hobby. And I was okay with that.

The Foundation Cracks

Zoom forward to the day, yes, the DAY, my world started to crumble. My husband had been unusually and increasingly sullen for at least a few months. He was not only withdrawing from me, but all of our kids. I suspected he might be having an affair, even though that went against everything I thought was in his character. However, I also knew that being Christian does not make one immune to temptation.

Deciding it was better to know than to continue guessing, I asked him point blank what was going on. I was shocked at his answer.

He was questioning his faith.

Boom! Just like that, everything turned upside down. Letting out his secret, he was no longer obligated to keep up the pretense of belief. For a short time, he continued to attend church but spoke openly about his disagreements with doctrine and traditions. Some nasty encounters occurred with a few church leaders. It got ugly.

It mortified me and confused the children. It would've been easier to accept if Hubby had simply quit going to services or gone to a different church, but he fought me on my spiritual beliefs and church responsibilities. He tried to derail any religious activity. I felt utterly betrayed. Without common foundational beliefs and goals, the trust and unity I relished in our family was shattered. Contention arose. We entered our dark ages.

Have you ever had a kick in the gut like that? Most likely you have, although it probably came in a different form. But no question, it hurts. It either leaves you sprawling in the dirt or you get up and keep pressing forward, even if you wobble. As for me? I staggered like a drunkard. At least on the inside. Outwardly, I forced a smile.

Shaky Ground

I had always said I was fully committed to our marriage unless he became unfaithful or abusive. For better or for worse, right? This was definitely a "for worse." But if my husband had lost his faith in what had been the very basis of our relationship, wasn't that being unfaithful?

I had to make some hard choices. After much fasting and prayer, I decided to stick with the marriage but also stay true to my faith. That was the first inkling of becoming a unipreneur. While Hubby chose to leave our mutually-agreed-upon path, I chose to continue following Christ. That meant living my passion in the same house as my dream-killer husband.

Then his trips, or "spiritual journeys" as he called them, started. He was a college professor, so he knew exactly when he had time off. Without consulting me, he went on various excursions around the country, delving into different religious traditions. During that first summer, he was gone for weeks at a time. I was left with all the children, not knowing for sure when or even if Daddy was coming home.

My hope was that in his searching, he would be like Dorothy in "The Wizard of Oz" and realize that he already had what he was looking for. That didn't happen. The kids couldn't understand what was going on, and I couldn't adequately answer their questions. I didn't understand it myself. My life became unpredictable and just plain weird. I quit journaling because it was too painful to write about what was happening to my family.

When Hubby's issues became open, most people from church treated me differently. They didn't mean to; it just happened. I think it's because they were so uncomfortable with my situation that they felt awkward and didn't know what to say. Neither did I. I understand their reactions now, but I didn't then. I felt truly abandoned, except for one dear friend that stuck with me for the first few years. Then she, too, left my life.

Our Dark Ages

The next several years are a blur. I do remember taking personal responsibility for my husband's choices. I got stuck in a negative loop, constantly asking myself what I could have done to prevent it or what I could do to fix it. Somehow it was all my fault.

I never quit going to church but it became rote. I went through the motions, wanting to set a good example for the children, but inside I felt ashamed and inadequate. While I prayed with the kids before meals and other occasions, I eventually quit my personal prayers. I didn't feel worthy.

Guilt and despair consumed me, but I faked being happy "for the kids' sake." I wasn't a conscious fraud, I deeply WANTED to feel joy. Interacting with our children was the only time I felt glimmers of happiness. However, the anguish was always simmering just below the surface.

My creative writing became non-existent. Sometimes as a temporary escape, as therapy, I would write deep, despairing thoughts, then tear them up so nobody could chance upon them. Over time, the negative loop turned into a complete downward spiral.

I tried desperately to be both Mom and Dad so the children wouldn't be deprived. Unfortunately, I overcompensated, which caused a whole different set of problems, but that's for another book. Seems ridiculous now, but that unhealthy thought process was my paradigm.

Even though my husband lived in the same house and provided for us financially, he was emotionally distant. He refused to step into our world, and the only time he accepted me was when I accompanied him into his. It was dark and awkward. It was foreign and counterfeit to my soul. I became a shadow of myself.

Then came my "dark night of the soul." Admittedly, if I didn't have such powerful love for our children, I might have taken my life. But I knew that ultimately, my death wouldn't solve anything, it would only cause suffering for those left behind. I just wanted the pain to stop.

So instead of downing that bottle of pills in my hand, I got on my knees, opening up in fervent prayer. I admitted that it was too much, too big, and I couldn't do it anymore. I literally turned everything over to God. A very loving, gentle Heavenly Father heard me. And He answered. I wasn't alone. The truth is, I had never been alone, but I had been too guilt-ridden to accept His grace.

The Light Shines

God's love and light was as brilliant as the darkness had been deep. It changed me. I forgave myself for mistakes; I let go of guilt and self-loathing. A quiet joy entered my heart for the first time in years. I realized my worth as a daughter of God and knew that my husband's choices had nothing to do with mine.

What a difference that one night's experience made! I had hit bottom and was bouncing back to life, to an authentic me. The road was still riddled with challenges, but I had the heart to face them. I would be a woman of faith, even if it meant standing alone.

Looking back, I'm sure my newfound strength didn't exactly thrill my hubby. He no longer had any control of me, even if that hadn't been his conscious intention. I returned to my path and mentally left him to wander his own. It didn't do much for our relationship. But it did wonders for me as an individual.

So how about you? Are you being your authentic self? Or are you squelching your growth, ignoring your passion because of someone else's choices? Only you can answer those questions, but please dig deep and be honest. You are only responsible for YOU.

Misguided Emotions

The next part of my journey tiptoed through the land of indignation and ire. I still played the blame game but instead of incriminating myself, I indicted my husband. He was the guilty party. My pain was his fault; so was the spiritual confusion in our family. I pumped all my energy into an attempt to be Supermom.

I literally said to myself, "They may have a crappy dad, but by gosh, they are going to have an awesome mom!" Of course, my definition of an awesome mom may not have been the same as our kids', but I did my best. I was a Girl Scout Leader, a 4-H Leader, a member of the Boy Scout Committee, headed fundraisers, taught Sunday School, etc., etc., etc. I was the one who baked cookies and birthday cakes and volunteered at events.

I became the woman who couldn't say no, cheerfully accepting requests from virtually anyone. Why? Because I subconsciously thought that throwing myself into service would somehow redeem me from my inner wrath and bitterness. In my world, Hubby's choices had blown apart the spiritual cohesion of our family. Resentment boiled in me like grease in a French fryer.

Guess you could say I was spiritually bipolar. I truly wanted to have Christlike characteristics, to be filled with compassion, understanding, forgiveness ... ah, forgiveness. That was the root of my quandary. As much as I had tried to dismiss it, the animosity toward my husband was still there. I still mourned the loss of my once "faithful, church-going" family.

Sweet Surrender

Intense inner turmoil isn't exactly healthy. If you could have touched my soul, it would have charred your fingertips! The searing rage that I tried so hard to stuff deep down inside me started eroding my health. Not fun. It took some pretty hard knocks before I finally acknowledged (again) that the problem was too massive for me to handle alone.

My conversation with God went something like this:

"Dear Heavenly Father, I can't this keep up. You know my longings and that I want to follow Christ's teachings. I want to be loving and kind, and yet, I have these horrible, ungodly feelings that constantly eat at me."

The still, small voice in my head said, "What would you have me do?"

"Please, please, please, just take away the anger. The resentment. The bitterness. I don't want it in my heart and I know you are the only one who can take it away."

The answer? "Then you must forgive him."

In my deepest core, I had known that was the answer all along, but it seemed too impossible to actually do.

"How?" I asked. "How can I forgive him when he isn't sorry, and the offense is still happening?"

"Because I forgive him."

I had to mull on that a while. Who was I to judge my husband? I can't get inside his head or his heart. I can only see the outward manifestations. And perhaps my perception of him as "the bad guy" was all wrong.

Did I like the results of his choices? No. But did he make those choices just to hurt me or our family? No. For the first time, I recognized that he didn't do it TO me. He did it FOR himself. Big difference.

And I'm sure if Hubby told "our story" it wouldn't sound anything like mine. Instead of him abandoning our initial path, he might see me as refusing to join him on a fresh, new course. Same picture, different viewpoint.

I remembered the statement attributed to Buddha: "Holding on to anger is like grasping a hot coal with the intent to throw it at someone else; you are the one who gets burned."

Actually, my husband probably did get a little toasted from my negativity towards him, but in reality, the third-degree burns were inside ME. And the truth was, I didn't want either of us to be in pain. I wanted us to be a happy family. And I still loved the old coot, dang it. Finally, I was ready to let go of the ire.

The retelling of this critical event in my life is a very condensed version, but the bottom line is, through God's help, I was able to forgive my hubby and truly love him again. I could see him as another child of God on his own hero's journey separate from mine. It freed me to move forward.

In your situation right now, is it possible that anger, resentment, and perhaps a lack of forgiveness are holding you back from reaching your potential? Are you willing to sacrifice animosity toward a dream-killer so that you may instead be filled with compassion? It's your choice.

I was so grateful for the new understanding that negative and positive emotions cannot occupy the same space. Choosing to see the good instead of dwelling on the bad brought peace and possibility back into my life.

Fast Forward

Our fifth child (middle daughter) was in her late teens at the time and introduced me to a multi-level marketing company (MLM). We sat in our living room where her upline showed me "The Plan." Much to their surprise, I registered. It was a no-brainer to me. I loved the products, the registration fee was ridiculously low, and the compensation plan made absolute sense. Most of all, I was ready to have "success" on my own, independent of my husband.

But the biggest boon didn't end up being the money (although that was great, too), but my own personal development. It's through this company that I was able to step up as a true unipreneur.

My hubby laughed when I first told him about the MLM. Not just an amused chuckle, but a "you've got to be kidding me, how could you be so stupid, it's a scam" belly-laugh. To make it worse, he made fun of me in front of the kids, and a couple of them joined in the mocking. I didn't react well at the time, but I also didn't let it stop me.

The following year I renewed with the company and, again, I got pummeled with derogatory speeches. "You haven't made big bucks yet, those so-called millionaires in your upline just want your money, you will never succeed ... yadda, yadda, yadda."

By that time, I was well-acquainted with some of those millionaires. They were compassionate, hard-working (but equally fun-loving) men and women who sincerely loved God, country, and their fellow man. Their organizations were so massive (and their passive income so huge) that they never needed to lift a finger again, but they DID. They still to this day do everything they can to help others achieve similar success. And their charitable donations? Oh. My. Goodness. They are the epitome of philanthropy. The last thing they needed was MY money.

Hubby's Truck

I pressed forward despite the eye-rolls, snickers, and full-blown tirades, not letting them demoralize or immobilize me. You'll learn more about that in Part I and II. Then came the summer that Hubby's pickup was about ready to give up the ghost. It still gives me grins.

My husband has never in his life bought a new vehicle (and I don't think he ever will). I'm okay with that. I fully understand his reasoning that a well-cared for, used vehicle makes good sense when you consider the depreciation of a new car as soon as you drive it off the dealership lot. I get it. So, from that standpoint, he was keeping his eye open for a dependable, used pickup.

One Saturday, I offered to accompany Hubby on his truck hunt. He showed me one at a local used car lot that he, admittedly, had already looked at twice. That was his top choice but also above his price range. As you read the following account of that day, please keep in mind, this was years ago, so the numbers seemed a lot bigger then.

"If that's the one you want, I think you should get it," I suggested.

Surprised but delighted, he started the process of ownership. They haggled on price and trade-in on his old truck until Hubby got it down to $14,000.

As we sat down to sign papers for a loan, I asked casually. "So how much if I pay cash?"

The dealer said, "Cash? Oh, uh ... I could knock off $1,000 ..."

"How about $10,000 total?" I asked.

"Um, how about $12,000?"

"How about $10,000 which includes all the tax, registration fee, and any other incidentals? I'll write you a check right now," I said, pulling out my business checkbook.

"$11,000. That's as low as I'll go."

I closed my checkbook. But before I could get it back into my purse, I heard the dealer's voice again.

"Okay, $10,000," he said, pushing his card in front of me so I knew how to make out the check. "You drive a hard bargain."

My husband didn't say a word until the moment the dealer took the paperwork back to his office.

"Do you really have $10,000 in your business account?" he whispered.

"Well, it's down $10,000 now but, yes."

"How much do you have in there?"

"More than enough to go buy me a car, too, if I want."

His eyes widened. "So how much do you have?"

"I'm not going to tell you."

"Why not?"

"Because I'm in a stupid, scam business that doesn't work," I replied sweetly.

He's never complained since. And currently, he's even a pretty good customer. But his name will never be added to my MLM. I truly love my husband, and we have an awesome life together now. But he isn't my business partner. I am, after all, a unipreneur.

The Upward Spiral Continues

I am a "lifer" with my MLM. Both my upline and my downline are like family to me. And three important principles I've learned through that association are: 1) spend your money wisely even when you have it to blow, 2) always be generous, and 3) once you get a profitable business established, invest the proceeds into developing other streams of income.

Several years ago, another dream seed took root: real estate investing. As a unipreneur, I started my own LLC and am happy to say it's doing well. I was able to utilize the principles I learned over a 10-year span in a much shorter time frame to achieve success. I want YOU to do the same.

More recently, I have rediscovered my original dream seed: being a word weaver. Having finished a novel and a screenplay, I realized I also have nonfiction in me that needs to be shared. I want to help others speed up their journeys toward living their passion even though they have dream-killers under the same roof.

That's why I'm writing this book – so you don't have to wallow through so much muck to get to the good stuff. I want YOU to achieve YOUR dreams! Are you ready?

I would suggest you start with Part I even if you've already shared your passion, your dream seed, with a loved one and had it stomped down. Carefully transplant that little seedling back into your heart, protect it from the dream-killers as you read through Part I. Implement what you learn and your dream seed will grow again.

As a side note, I will be using the masculine terms "he" and "his" when referring to dream-killers but that in no way indicates that they're all male. It's strictly for ease and consistency in writing. I find the message gets bogged down when attempting to alternate "he" and "she" or writing "his/hers" each time. Hope you don't mind.

I'm so excited for you to pursue your passion, develop your gift, and share it with the world. I wish you all the best on your journey!

PART I
PREPARE

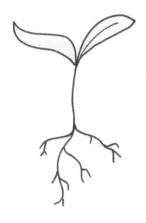

Inward Germination

Before sharing your passion with others (especially those who are potential dream-killers), you must prepare mentally. The dream seed must be nurtured and sheltered as it sprouts into a fragile little seedling. In this section, I will share ways to protect the dream internally as it strengthens, before sharing it outwardly.

CHAPTER 1

CLARIFY YOUR VISION

"Begin with the end in mind."

—Stephen R. Covey

What is it you want? It isn't enough to say, "I want to be rich" or "I want to be healthy" or "I want to help other people." No one, including yourself, will take you seriously and the dream-killers will have fuel for their ridicule. Get specific. With clarity of vision comes increased passion for your dream.

Take a block of time to be alone, uninterrupted, so you can clear your mind from outward distractions as well as your own mental chatter. That isn't easy, I know. Eastern cultures refer to it as the "jumping monkey" that is constantly vying for your attention. Tether the monkey. Or let it swing on a tree in the back yard.

Personally, I pray, ponder, meditate – whatever it takes to get "in the flow." Instrumental music playing softly in the background quickens the time for me to get in tune with myself.

And yes, I noticed the pun. When clearing my mind, I don't listen to songs with vocals because I find myself singing along with them, even if only mentally. But that's just me.

Other times I put on an audio of nature sounds like a babbling brook, waterfall, or gentle rain. I also like the faint sound of the ocean, but I find if the waves are crashing too loudly or there are seagulls squawking, I tense up. Same with birds in a rainforest. Droplets of water splashing on the canopy of trees? Yes. Parrots and toucans? Not so much.

So, what would trigger you into an open, contemplative state? If you already have a method, awesome! If not, you might try my suggestions or experiment with your own ideas. Perhaps Beethoven soothes you. Or it might make you feel like you're in a dentist's office. Lyrics in a song might not distract you like they do me. What about the sounds of a thunderstorm? Or you might prefer silence.

The important thing is to discover what works for YOU. And block out time to make it happen.

I find these "in flow" experiences to be an unlikely blend of energy and calmness. If you haven't already experienced it, you'll understand what I'm talking about when you do. While you're in that receptive mental state, envision what your dream seed will grow to be. Ask yourself questions.

For example (continuing with the seed analogy), you might ask:

- Will it be a rosebush? Red or pink? Yellow, maybe?
- Will it be a mighty oak tree with a tire swing hanging from a lower branch?

- What about an English ivy growing up the walls of a stately stone mansion?
- Will it bear fruit like apples or raspberries?
- Will it delight the eye like a Japanese dogwood or a burning bush?
- Will it be a willow tree gracing the edge of a winding stream?

Get the picture? Yes, another pun. The more vividly you paint the mental image, the faster your heart beats, the quicker your breath. And this isn't a one-time occurrence. Set time for these vision-quest experiences on a regular basis. As you do, your dream will not only flourish but proliferate.

So, what will YOUR life look like when your passion is fulfilled? How will it feel sitting in the theater, your amazed dream-killer in the seat beside you, watching your hit Broadway play? Imagine yourself bending over to have the gold medal slipped around your neck, hearing your national anthem being played in the background. Picture a million dollars on your business bank statement or see yourself handing a check for $100,000 to your favorite nonprofit organization.

What does your designed life look like to YOU?

Write It Down

Writing down your dream, especially by hand, can have a profound mental impact. Both experience and science back this claim.

When you visualize your goals and dreams, it stimulates the right hemisphere of your brain, the imaginative center. The act of writing it down activates the left hemisphere, the logical side. Blending the two together, especially on a continuing basis, grounds the vision and turns your brain into a powerhouse of possibility.

Don't believe me? Google it. Or better yet, try it out and see for yourself.

Another advantage to writing down what you visualize is that it opens up your subconscious to notice opportunities that you may have been too preoccupied to notice before. You will also become aware of new ones as they arise.

It's my opinion that God put us in a magnificent and abundant universe that is filled with the absolute possibility to achieve ANYTHING we desire that is good and expansive. Yes, we all have unique talents and abilities. Yes, we all have certain mental and physical limitations. But ANYONE can use whatever resources are available in their particular realm to improve themselves. And "ANYONE" includes YOU!

By clarifying your vision and writing it down, you can speed up the process.

Another vital point to clarifying your dream is that it identifies and magnifies your "why." It will become evident for what or for whom you are doing this. Is it for personal growth? For your family's benefit? For the betterment of your community or even mankind as a whole? There are no right or wrong answers to these questions, and it is an individual journey.

Thinking and writing. Pondering and putting it to paper. It is a very illuminating process.

Personally, I have a dream journal containing handwritten lists of what I would love in my life. There are four lists:

1. Things I would love to do
2. Things I would love to have
3. Places I would love to go
4. The Person I would love to BE

As I achieve one dream, another bigger one builds on it or replaces it. My dream journal is always expanding because I am expanding.

I also have what some would call a vision board directly above the desk in my office. It has pictures of horses and eagles which have deep meaning for me. There are clippings of various cruises, photos of family, and index cards with quotes and scriptures. Near the center is a tiny construction paper heart that says, "I love you Gram." The predominate wording that catches my eye are the words in all caps, "A QUITTER NEVER WINS – AND A WINNER NEVER QUITS!"

So, what gets your heart pumping and your juices flowing? Imagine it. Write it down. Keep it growing.

Don't Get Stuck in the "How"

While it's important to know the "what" and your "why", you don't have to know the "how." Truth is, if you already know the exact steps to accomplish your passion, then it probably isn't a very big dream.

And, by the way, there's nothing wrong with that. It's better to have a small dream than no dream at all, but hopefully it is just part of a bigger picture. A much bigger picture.

If you have a rigid, detailed plan on how to attain your ultimate goal, it closes your mind to opportunities that may pop up along the way that would speed up the process or expand the end result. So, the trick is to have clarity of vision without clutching the details so tightly that it chokes out an even greater outcome.

Think of it this way: being too stuck on the details may block your dream seed from a healthy dose of plant food that unexpectedly presents itself. When seeing or saying your dream, I suggest adding "this or something even better!"

So, have your end in mind and step toward it. But be open to new possibilities along the way.

Have you ever gone tent camping?

Okay, that may seem like a random question, but hear me out. I have been on many campouts with little people so the following story is not an unusual occurrence.

Whether or not you've been in the woods at night, pretend that you are asleep in a tent with a 5-year-old in the outer unit of a Scout camp. At 3:17 a.m., a little finger pokes you and a wee voice whispers, "I gotta go potty."

You have two choices. You can ignore the voice and go back to sleep (give up on your passion) in which case, you may find yourself in a wet and messy situation in the morning (regret). Or, you can make your way to the nearest latrine which is 50 yards away, down a winding dirt path in the woods.

In the comfort of your toasty sleeping bag, it would be much easier to stay horizontal (pretend your passion doesn't exist). But deep down inside, you know you will be sorry if you go back to sleep. And besides ... that 5-year-old probably isn't going to let you settle back down anyway (your dream seed is germinating).

So you decide to get up (commit to your dream). That means flipping on your flashlight (awareness), putting on shoes and bug repellent (preparing the best you can for whatever lies ahead), and getting out of the tent (leaving your comfort zone).

You know you want to arrive safely at the latrine (your destination) but don't know exactly how to move down the darkened path (your own hero's journey). Your child who desperately needs to go potty (your clarified, written dream) is giving you a sense of urgency to move ahead.

There is no moon peeking through the trees to guide you. The ray streaming from the flashlight only illuminates a few feet ahead, but as you take a step, more of the path is shown (the steps on your journey are revealed to you one at a time as you move forward). As the light shines on a fallen log, you step over it; when it beams on a possum, you wait for a few moments for it to shuffle off into the woods (you become aware of obstacles, including your dream-killers, and how to handle each one of them).

Yay! Your little one gets to the latrine in time (success!) And in both cases, the trip to the potty (and your journey to your dream), there is an increasing sense of accomplishment and gratitude as you get closer to the fulfillment of your vision! Life is wonderful!

It doesn't matter if you start on your path with a glow stick, a flashlight, or a flood lamp, the important thing is to make a move in the right direction. You don't need to have the whole map in front of you, just the next step. Keep moving forward, one action at a time. You may be tempted to wander off on a side path, or get distracted by fireflies, or discouraged by a dream-killer. But if you stick to your clarified, written vision, you will eventually get where you want to go.

Live from Your Vision

When you have clarity of vision, you know what type of person you will need to BE to enjoy that success. Don't wait for your dream seed to become a full-grown sequoia to BE that person. BEcome that confident, grateful, compassionate person NOW.

Besides my dream journal and vision board, I also have what I call my vision statement. It's written on an index card that I carry around in my purse. I usually read it (often out loud) every morning, every night, and sometimes in between. It is a fluid statement. That is, it changes and adapts as I grow and expand my dream.

While no two people's vision is exactly the same, I'm going to open up a vein here and share with you my current vision statement as an example. It doesn't contain any details of the ultimate life I imagine, but it's a statement of who I want to BE. Here it goes:

"I am a creative, grateful, infinite daughter of God and a beacon of light who continually learns, grows, connects, and serves. I have the power within me to design the life I absolutely love living, by the thoughts I manifest and the daily actions I take. Each day, I'm unleashing my infinite light for the benefit of myself, my family, my friends, my loved ones, and anyone accepting of my positive influence. This or something even better. And so it is."

Reading my vision statement helps keep me on my desired course or pull me back in line when I drift. And you know what? It works. I purposely added the word "usually" when I said I read it every day. Unfortunately, there are days when I get distracted and forget. After all, I'm so very human.

When I feel blah or overwhelmed or annoyed – any of those negative, icky emotions that I used to blame on circumstances – I can now recognize as a meandering from my vision statement. I had temporarily lost focus on BEing the person of my utmost success. So, without beating up myself for slipping, I switch my thoughts and actions back on track.

You can do it, too.

Include Your Dream-killer

While you are in the process of clarifying your vision, remember to guard your dream seed carefully. Don't share it just yet. Or if you already have and received a negative response, withdraw it back to the safety of your protection.

But that doesn't mean you have to cut yourself off from the dream-killer in your house. Quite the contrary. It's time to reach out to him, soften him up a bit, but perhaps not the way you'd expect.

Instead of telling him about your dream, ask about his.

Give it a try. He may not respond at first. Or he may look at you like you're crazy. Perhaps he purposely buried his dream out of fear or deep disappointment. In that case, he might get annoyed or even mad. Just back off and try a little later with an adapted approach. Don't give up.

Remember the suggestion to get "in the zone" and ask yourself intriguing questions to clarify your vision? It works with other people, too.

The most successful method I have used with several dream-killers and indifferent family members is to ask questions. Here are some that resulted in deep and fruitful conversations:

- If you could travel any place in the world, where would you go?
- If you could own your own business, what would it be?
- If you could build your perfect house, what would it look like?
- If you had all the time and money you wanted, what would you do?

Get the idea?

Frankly, I expect negative responses at first because dream-building is such a foreign concept to people without personal vision. Immediate reactions have been "I can't afford that; I don't have the time; I don't have the experience; I don't know the right people; I'm too old; I don't have enough education; I'm too busy ... blah, blah, blah."

In my head, I'm thinking, "Excuses, excuses! I know you have dream seeds, divine gifts to share! You can do this, I know you can." Outwardly, I keep smiling and love the person despite their initial resistance to rediscovering their passion.

Back when my husband was still ranting about my MLM business, I distinctly remember him saying, "They're just a bunch of dream-peddlers! They're just trying to sell hope!"

I thought, "How sad that he puts a negative spin on everything. We are dream-builders, not dream-peddlers. We don't sell hope, we give hope. Not false hope but a real hope of building a better life." I had not yet experienced success with that business, but I recognized the potential and flourished in the possibilities.

And I haven't given up on Hubby. He still isn't a dream-builder but he's much less of a dream-killer than he used to be. He's now more of a dream-observer.

How about your dream-killer? I'll bet you know what he likes. You know his hot buttons. Does he like cars or motorcycles? Does he like to travel? Is he into golfing, gardening, or gaming? Encourage him to talk about what he likes. It may surprise you. It may surprise you both.

When he starts talking? Listen! Don't dilute his story by interspersing yours. Only share your dream when and if he invites you to do so. Remember, you can't expect him to get excited about your dreams if you don't care about his. Don't pretend to be interested, BE interested. Just because you love him.

Want an example?

My husband is an avid bicyclist. As in he loves to ride 30-40 miles every day that the weather is good and does 100-mile tours with his bike club.

Me? It hurts just to think of a 100-mile ride. I've never had good experiences with bicycles. My tail end has always been sore both during and after; bikes just aren't my "thing." I'd much rather be on a horse.

A few weeks ago, Hubby and I were walking down a clearance aisle at the local Walmart. He picked up a bicycle helmet, carefully inspected it, and exclaimed, "This is a good helmet – I can't believe it's so cheap. It's way too little for me, but it would fit you perfectly."

Then without even looking at me, he set the helmet back on the shelf and muttered under his breath, "I wish you'd ride with me."

He didn't know I heard him, but my heart twanged. Evidently it was something important to him. I inhaled deeply, picked up the helmet, and flipped it around in my hands.

"Which is the front?" I asked, chuckling at my obvious inexperience.

He put it on my head and adjusted the strap, a glimmer of hope in his eyes. "If you have a bike that fits, it will be a whole different experience."

I held my breath for a moment, trying to get up the courage to commit. It was reeeaaallly hard for me.

"You don't have to go on tours. Just start with a mile. I'll be right there with you," he added.

"Okay. You get me a bike that fits, and I'll ride with you."

I wish you could have seen the grin on his face. He started telling me all sorts of biking tips and how much fun we'll have and ... and ... and ...

It gave me joy because it gave him joy. He's already measured me so that he can get the perfect bike. I will be open-minded and accept the possibility that I can enjoy bike riding. After all, I am now committed.

So, what can you do to draw closer to your dream-killer on his turf? It doesn't have to be huge, even little things will help you connect.

And little things added together can have huge results.

There is one more thing I would like to mention about attempting to get your dream-killer to consider his hidden dream seeds.

What if he won't engage in a dream-building conversation? Or what if he's a total grump about it? Please, please, please, try not to take it personally. His dream seed might be so withered or moldy or buried so deep, he forgot he had one. Give him time. Give him space. But every now and then, try again. Sprinkle a little water on the dream seeds and just like yours, they may start to stir.

ACTION STEPS

For Your Passion:

- Get a clear mental picture of what your dream will look like, realizing that it will be even bigger and better than you now imagine.
- Try starting a dream journal and/or a vision board.
- Write down your vision statement and read it daily, thus retraining your brain for success.
- BE the person you envision living in your passion.

For Your Relationships:

- Without revealing YOUR dream, ask your dream-killer questions that might ignite HIS hidden dreams.
- Listen carefully to what he shares and support his interests.

CHAPTER 2

BRIGHTEN YOUR ATTITUDE

*"Within each of us lies the power of our consent to
health and sickness, to riches and poverty,
to freedom and to slavery.
It is we who control these, and not another."*

—Richard Bach

I grew up in North Texas. Four of our six children were born there, too. Besides withstanding scorching heat, snake encounters, and chigger bites (if you don't know what a chigger is, feel fortunate), living in North Texas also means membership in Tornado Alley.

I've seen several twisters but, unlike Dorothy, I haven't actually been "in" one. Knock on wood.

However, I have seen the devastation they can cause. Huge trees uprooted, farm machinery bent up like pretzels, whole communities turned to rubble ... the power is dumbfounding. No one can control a tornado or the destruction it can cause, but you CAN choose how you will react in its wake.

Case in point: After becoming more aware of the power of attitude, I watched a news report on a tornado that absolutely demolished a small town. Miraculously, no one had been killed, and there were only minor injuries.

The reporters interviewed two couples whose homes were reduced to heaping piles of broken brick and splintered wood. The differences were stark.

The first couple was understandably heartbroken. The man poked a stick in the debris, turning chunks of it over as if some treasure might be found underneath. He muttered constantly, shaking his head in angered disbelief.

And the woman. The best description I can think of is "weeping, wailing, and gnashing of teeth."

When the reporter stuck the microphone in the wife's face, she sobbed, "We have nothing left! We lost everything."

The husband stood near her, stick still in hand, agreeing, "It's all gone. I don't know what we'll do."

I'm sure there were other viewers like me, who cried at their anguish.

Then came the second couple. They stood on top of the wreckage, side by side, taking in the devastation.

The news reporter trudged his way through the mess, mic in hand. When he prompted a reaction, they gave an unexpected response. Taking each other's hand, the husband and wife actually smiled.

"We aren't even hurt," the woman replied, looking up at her companion. "We still have each other."

He returned her adoring gaze and waved his hand toward the rubble. "We'll just rebuild. Not exactly sure how, but we'll find a way."

"A new adventure," she added. They embraced, still smiling.

"Yep," he laughed. "It'll be quite an adventure!"

What do you think was the difference between the two couples experiencing basically the same thing?

Attitude. New adventure? Or death sentence. It is a matter of choice.

It's the same with your passion.

YOU Are the Authority of YOU

You may not always (if ever) be able to control the circumstances around you, particularly the actions of your dream-killers, but you CAN always control what goes on in your mind. You are the ruler in that realm. No one can usurp that power without your permission.

Does that surprise you?

It did me when I first heard the idea. Thoughts had just popped into my head according to what was going on around me. That's just the way life worked. Or so I assumed.

Just like the first lady in the tornado story, if something LOOKED devastating, then it WAS devastating. The outside conditions determined what I thought and felt, which in turn, affected the action (or non-action) I took. That was my truth. I didn't know I had a choice.

Now, however, because I've become more aware of the power within each one of us, I have more control.

You can, too.

It isn't that I turn a blind eye. I don't deny or ignore the physical facts. And I certainly don't stuff them deep inside me anymore - that can cause all sorts of physical and mental ailments, especially when built up over a long period of time. But I don't embrace the negative facts either. I recognize them and let their power pass by without messing with my head.

Just like the second lady in the tornado story, I say, "Yep. That was quite a storm, alright. It may take a while to recover but I will find a way. And I'll keep on enjoying life as I do it!"

As Eleanor Roosevelt so succinctly stated, "All the water in the world can't drown you unless it gets inside of you."

Many people in today's world are stuck in a victim complex. I used to be, too. My thinking was, "I can't do this because someone did that." It was mostly my dream-killer's fault, don't you know.

Boo-hoo.

Not any longer. Now in my life, V stands for Victor, not victim.

How about in yours? If you currently let your dream-killer rule you, I challenge you to get rid of the "I can't because …" syndrome and exchange it with "I can, and I will find a way …".

If you view yourself as successful with your passion and act accordingly, you'll be able to recognize opportunities that you probably won't notice if you are stuck in a woe-is-me attitude.

Thanks to the Internet (Yay, Internet!), we now have access to virtually limitless personal stories that can inspire us to overcome what we see as limitations. Visit www.UnipreneurBook.com to find an ever-growing list of people who have overcome severe obstacles to achieve amazing results.

In addition, I suggest you also search for other accounts that will encourage you on your specific journey. I would love for you to share them with me.

As a matter of fact, I would love for you to share YOUR success story, too! Keep nurturing your dream seed. It WILL flourish, even beyond what you are now imagining.

In 2016, I had the privilege of speaking with the actor, Lou Ferrigno (who played The Incredible Hulk in the old TV series) near Buffalo, NY. Lou had 80 percent hearing loss as a child, but that didn't stop him from following his passion. I'll never forget his words to the audience, "You only get out of life what you put into it." Those are great words to live by!

If you can't change something, I hope you choose to live with it peaceably instead of revving up the negative charge.

Plant Your Dream Seeds in Good Soil

Just like pumpkin seeds won't grow in a toxic garden, neither will dream seeds thrive in a toxic mind.

In the Bible (Matthew 13:1-23), Jesus shares a parable about a person sowing seeds. Some of the seeds fall inadvertently along the way and birds gobble them up. Others fall on stony ground where there isn't much dirt to get the roots established. Plants spring up, but the scorching sun withers them away. Other seeds fall among thorns and get choked. And finally, some seeds are sown carefully in good soil, which result in a bountiful harvest.

His awesome analogy also applies to dream seeds. Think about it.

If you carelessly throw out a dream seed, chances are a dream-killer is going to swoop down and chew it up. If you toss it onto a stony place where it doesn't get rooted and established, then when the challenges arise (and they will), the sprout will wither and die. Plant it with the mindset that the dream-killers in your house are correct when they ridicule you, the dream seed will get choked out of existence.

Ah, but sow your dream seed in a mind that is cultivated with a bright, cheerful attitude ever-seeking the good, and it will flourish!

Pull up the weeds of doubt and fear as soon as you recognize them. Keep a vigilant eye so the dream-killers don't attack it when it's still tiny and vulnerable. Nurture and protect your passion as it grows and strengthens. Keep it rooted in the rich, deep garden of your empowered mind.

Okay, that sounds great, but how in the heck do you actually apply it in your own life? What prepares the mind to be a fertile place for dream seeds?

For me, the most powerful way to brighten my attitude is to constantly be aware of my blessings. I focus on giving thanks.

Did you start your dream journal yet? If not, stop reading right now and get to it! If you did, add another section called "my gratitude list."

Remember the potency of thinking AND writing (with your own hand, not a word processor)? That applies here, too.

I found the process of listing my gratitudes easy at first. I started with the biggies like our children and my faith, my parents and siblings, a roof over my head and food in the fridge. But as the flurry of obvious blessings in my life slowed, I started to think deeper. And deeper. And deeper.

For instance, at first, I wrote that I was grateful for my physical senses. Later I listed them separately. Then I broke it down even further. Instead of just "sight," I added that I was thankful for colors, patterns, landscapes, seascapes, watching movies, observing a chipmunk scampering in the backyard, soaking in the brilliant orange and red flames of a setting sun, studying my grandbaby's sweet little face as she sleeps in my arms ....

Get it?

I have pages and pages, two to three columns on front and back, and I still add to it. Besides the lists, I now have a section in back of the binder where I add paragraphs about things, people, or moments in time that deserve more detail than just a word or phrase.

It's very hard to have a grateful heart AND a sour attitude.

While my expanding gratitude list isn't something I read or add to every day, it's always there when I am tempted to give in to something negative. It lifts me.

There are daily habits, however, that truly help me keep a continually bright attitude. Before I get out of bed each morning, sometimes even before I open my eyes, I make a mental list of blessings and thank God for each specific one. I give Him the glory. I do the same thing before going to bed at night.

If I'm having a particularly challenging day, and I don't have access to my dream journal, I may hand-write a physical list of blessings, too. This has kept me cool and on track in circumstances in which my former self would have exploded in a torrent of tears.

By the way, please don't think I'm saying I'm perfect in this. I still have lousy days. But they are fewer and very far between. My highs are higher and my lows are higher, too.

And when I do have a rotten day, I still give a prayer of gratitude before I go to sleep, acknowledge the negative, and then release it. I don't beat myself up over it; I just let it go and start fresh the next morning.

The point is to change daily habits to positive ones. It may be hard at first, but it gets easier and easier until it becomes second nature. Even seemingly small positive changes can bring huge results in your life over time. The more dedicated and focused you are on switching to good habits, the steeper your upward path.

Music to My Ears

Not too long ago, I had a challenging conversation with one of our children, a teenager. Instead of giving in to the anger and frustration that was pounding to get into my head, I turned on Mozart and started mopping the kitchen floor.

Frankly, I don't often listen to classical music and I rarely mop during the day. I do it at night when there isn't traffic so the floor can dry without footprints. And it wasn't even on my to-do list for another week.

Within minutes, I was actually enjoying the task, swirling the mop in exaggerated motions as the notes crescendoed. I let the music flow through me, washing the icky emotions right into the mop water.

Unexpectedly, my husband showed up at the door, giving me a strange look.

I laughed, pointed to the bedroom of the offending child, and said, "It's just been a Mozart kind of morning."

Music can speak to your soul if you let it. What type of music moves you?

Me? It depends on my mood. Or perhaps more accurately stated, the mood I want to create.

I have playlists with everything from Rock to Country to Irish Pub songs, and, yes, even Classical. I have Gospel, New Age, Reggae, and Ambient. I listen to instrumentals and vocals, soloists, bands, choirs, whatever moves me in the direction I want to go in that moment.

And I sing. Not in public. After all, I try my best to be considerate of others. But I sing in the car, in the shower, in the backyard, wherever I'm alone and have the desire to express the love and gratitude in my heart or release something negative.

I'm not just talking about a hymn of praise, although I sing those, too. But even silly camp songs bring me joy. Have you ever tried to sing a song like "Herman the Worm" and be grumpy? I don't think it's humanly possible.

I have sung "Herman the Worm" in my head when my dream-killer was encroaching on my peace. It worked. As a matter of fact, his huffing completely stopped because I started smiling for no apparent reason.

Some exceptions must be given here about the "I don't sing in public" statement. I love to sing in church choirs or around a campfire. But I don't generally do solos, except when singing kids to sleep at night. Luckily, as far as I know, it has never induced nightmares.

I also have a few family members and friends with whom I break out in spontaneous song. The joy just bubbles out. It doesn't happen very often but when it does, it's AWESOME!

Once it happened in an elevator at an MLM convention. One of my upline and I were sandwiched in with other business owners (most of whom I didn't know yet) when the doors opened to reveal two people desperate to get 10 floors down to the lobby. There was hesitancy because we were already packed.

We all scrunched in closer and someone said, "Come on, get in. We're all family!"

Without even looking at each other, my upline and I started singing "We are faaaaamily! I got all my sisters with me ..." It was as if we had been cued - we were perfectly synchronized.

By the time we reached the lobby, almost all (if not all) our fellow travelers were singing with us. We may have been sardines for that 10-floor journey, but we were happy sardines. Everyone left the elevator still humming or laughing. Our attitudes were definitely brightened.

So, do you sing? I challenge you to add it to your arsenal of pick-me-ups. If you feel you can't sing, then hum. At least give it a try.

My dad whistled. Not like the loud, annoying whistle through my teeth that I used when I called my horse, but amazingly intricate tunes with crescendos and trills that mesmerized me. I can still hear it in my head. The memory brings a warm flood of peace and contentment. So, is all whistling music? Definitely not! My dad's? Absolutely!

If you are fortunate enough to play an instrument, that's another way to lift your spirits. I'm not an accomplished musician by any means, but I know enough to play basics on a piano and harp. When I practice, it may not be music to anyone else's ears, but it's a venue for me to release negative energy and replace it with positive.

My husband also bought me an exquisitely hand-carved African drum called a Djembe. Besides being eye-candy, it's fun to tap. It doesn't sound like a kid banging on a pot with a wooden spoon, either, even when I'm the one beating it. The deep, resonating tones are very pleasing.

You might consider getting one, too. Or something similar. Whatever resonates with YOU. And, yes, pun intended.

The final "music" I want to mention is laughter. It may seem obvious that this would brighten an attitude, but I know in my personal dark ages, the pain was so great that authentic laughter was in starvation mode. If not starvation, then certainly malnutrition.

Genuine laughter doesn't have to be loud and boisterous to be healing. Even a brief chuckle provides a boost of endorphins.

One of my favorite quotes is from a sweet but feisty woman, now gracing Heaven, named Marjorie Pay Hinckley. She said, "The only way to get through life is to laugh your way through it. You either have to laugh or cry. I prefer to laugh. Crying gives me a headache."

Who in their right mind would want a headache??? Choose to lighten up.

Habits or Have-To's

Yes, I know I talked about habits just a few pages back. However, it warrants more discussion so please bear with me.

Each of us was born with certain personality traits and behavioral tendencies. But does that mean if you have a proclivity to feel or act a certain way that you can't change it?

Or could it, perhaps, just be a habit? Really think about it.

As an example, for almost a half century, I reacted to many things with tears. If I was happy or sad, I cried. If I was angry, frustrated, grumpy, excited, blissful, embarrassed, I cried. If somebody looked at me cross-eyed, I cried. I was a real, honest-to-goodness Blubber-Bear. Frankly, I thought it was in my DNA. It's just the way I was made.

Then I discovered the possibility that my tearfulness could just be a habit. Did I react with tears because ... well, because that's what I'd always done? My brain was wired to cry, but could I consciously re-wire it?

In short, the answer was YES! Tears are no longer my first reaction to every emotion.

Do I still cry? Of course! But only when it serves my highest good. I sometimes shed tears of gratitude or joy, especially when I pray or have tender moments with a family member. I cry when friends and family pass from this earthly plane because it helps process the grief and transition to life without them. I had several tearful downpours when we had to put my dog down last summer - from the moment we made the difficult decision until several days after her death.

There are still times when I have tears, but the tears no longer have me. I made a conscious choice to feel and act certain ways and release others I didn't want. I broke the Blubber-Bear habit.

What does all this have to do with brightening your attitude?

Attitude, too, is a result of habit. We expect certain results because that's been the track record. But your attitude can change. Our history doesn't have to define who we are or how we respond at this very moment.

Okay, so your dream-killer has made you feel angry or bitter or worthless or stupid or ... whatever.

Newsflash: He didn't MAKE you feel that way. You LET him. Even if you didn't realize you had a choice, you did. And then it became a habit.

The great news is, that also means you have the power to NOT feel angry or bitter or worthless or stupid or ... whatever. You can break that habit of allowing your dream-killer to control your thoughts, feelings, and/or actions.

It isn't easy to do at first. Like with anything, it takes conscious, consistent effort over time before a new habit replaces an old one, but it is so liberating when you master it!

If you choose to have a positive attitude, then you will. I know you can!

The next question is, what habits can you change to improve your relationship with your dream-killer? Do you expect unpleasant encounters and bring along boxing gloves or a tissue box because you already know how you're going to react?

Remember, if you want things to change for the better, you can't keep doing the same old, same old.

Switch things up.

Instead of expecting the worst, expect the best. Instead of dwelling on what you see as his faults, look for the good things he does. If you get stuck, remember why you got together with him in the first place and accentuate those traits.

Recall the awesome feelings that gratitude invokes? It will for him, too. Trade the criticism (even if you only think it) for outward praise. Catch him doing something you appreciate and tell him.

"That was a great pizza. Thanks for picking it up!"

"I love the way you get the bills paid on time each month. I know it's a pain, but I'm grateful you get it done."

"Thank you for putting out the trash each week, I really appreciate it!"

Now don't be a phony. If he only takes out the trash when he feels like it, which is once a month at best, then the above sentence would be taken as sarcasm. The point is to seek the good, and overlook the not-so-good.

In closing this chapter, I'd like to remind you that you have the power in you to control your thoughts and feelings. While you may not control all your circumstances, you can control how you react or respond to them. These are divine gifts to humankind.

Life is filled with gifts. Whether we recognize or accept them is a different matter. Contemplation on good gifts, no matter how small, brings peace and joy to the heart. And sincere gratitude opens the floodgates to even more.

ACTION STEPS

For Your Passion:

- Make the commitment that you will concentrate on positive things in your life and release the power of the negative ones that you can't change.

- Visit www.UnipreneurBook.com to find an ever-growing list of people who have overcome severe challenges to achieve amazing results. Read their stories and/or watch their videos. You can expand this by doing research yourself. Feel free to share them!

- Add a gratitude list to your dream journal. Start by listing the first 100 things that come to mind—no matter how big or small.

- While at www.UnipreneurBook.com, check out the music section, too. I've even included a video of "Herman the Worm" to encourage a smile. Feel free to sing along.

For Your Relationships:

- Pick a genre of music that you and your dream-killer BOTH enjoy. Find a time to listen to it together or perhaps go to a concert. If either of you (or both), play an instrument, make time to share it. OR watch a funny movie or comedy act together.

- To get in the habit of accentuating the best, for the next 3 weeks, find at least three things a day that you can tell your dream-killer you appreciate about him. These don't have to be new ones each day- repeats are acceptable as long as they are sincere!

CHAPTER 3

TWEAK YOUR PERSPECTIVE

*"If the doors of perception were cleansed,
everything would appear to man as it is – infinite."*

—William Blake

A couple of weeks ago, I was sitting in a school parking lot, waiting for our youngest daughter. I was using the time to check my email when a woman pulled up a couple of spaces away. I wondered why she didn't park next to me, then I noticed that her car was crooked.

"Oh," I thought. "She must have come in at a funny angle and didn't want to scratch my car."

I went back to my email when another car pulled in on the other side of her. Then another. And another. They were all askew. I looked at the car on the other side of me and had a sudden realization.

"They aren't parked crooked," I breathed. "I am!"

53

I promptly started the engine, pulled my car back, and parked straight.

From my initial point of view, everyone else was parked catawampus. It took considering a different perspective to get myself in alignment.

Have you ever had that happen?

Because we are each standing in a different spot on this earth, no two people see things from exactly the same viewpoint. Add to that our unique genetic make-up as well as individualized experiences - that means an infinite number of possible views.

Some people seem to live their whole lives from a very narrow perspective and don't even bother trying to understand others. I pity them. It must be very frustrating and contractive to constantly think everyone else is parked crooked.

Narrow-minded people can't live a life of passion because they are limited by a mental prison that they build and guard themselves. They don't respect differing beliefs or embrace change. They often live in the past rather than enjoying the present. A life of criticism, harsh judgment, missed opportunities, and stagnation. So sad.

This isn't you! Otherwise, you wouldn't be exploring ways to live your passion in a house full of dream-killers. You would have given up long ago.

By opening our minds to different perspectives, we can increase our understanding of others. It increases our curiosity, broadens our thinking, helps us embrace change and try new things. It not only helps us find solutions to problems, but it turns those problems into opportunities. It's an ever-upward spiral.

Expanded Awareness

Now please don't misunderstand me. I don't suggest being so open-minded that your brain falls out.

Understanding and accepting another person's viewpoint does NOT mean you have to adopt their belief system. But you can have a strong opposing opinion without disrespecting the other person's supposition. If we were like robots, all programmed exactly the same, life would be very boring and pointless.

And sometimes, it's good to change parking spots. Or even go to a different lot all together. Take some time to observe other drivers and see what you can learn.

For example, I have close friends and family at vastly differing points on the political spectrum. Many believe the polar opposite of what I do. It used to bug me because I couldn't fathom their thinking. Now, however, I understand that our political beliefs are, in part, offspring of our individual experiences, interpretations of history (including religion), and personal visions of the future.

In other words, we come from a wide range of perspectives. So, it's possible for two people to have clashing political views and still both be "good" people.

To illustrate this, I'm going to share two personal stories about a currently very controversial issue. Abortion.

Whatever your position is, please bear with me. This is not about getting you to change your core beliefs. It is about learning to look at the world through someone else's eyes.

Several years ago, I shared a Pro-Life meme on my personal Facebook page. A fellow Girl Scout leader that I had worked with for almost 10 years pulled me aside before a planning meeting and said, "I'm so disappointed in you. All these years I thought you were a really nice person. But you're just a fake."

I had no idea what she was talking about. When I asked her what I did that wasn't "nice", she referred to the meme.

"If you aren't Pro-Choice, then you don't care about the plight of teen mothers, or children who are abused or abandoned because their moms didn't want them. You don't care about poverty or starvation because you care more about controlling someone else's body. If you aren't Pro-Choice, you don't have a heart."

I was floored.

I was born with a tender heart. I don't take credit for it, that was a gift from God. It's in my very nature to care deeply about every living creature ... two-legged and four-legged, furry, feathered, scaled, or bare-skinned. I've even been known to carry spiders outside of the house rather than squish them. And I stop my car to take turtles across the road.

And people. Oh. My. Gosh. To say I didn't care about relief from suffering - well, my heart was aching so badly at that moment, I thought it would burst. Strange, since apparently, I didn't have one.

Furthermore, I had no desire to control ANYONE except myself. ALL lives mattered to me (and still do) regardless of color, gender, ability, nationality, age ... including the pre-born!

At that point in time, I still held the belief that circumstances determined what I felt, so I did what my history dictated. I cried. I couldn't even go to the planning meeting. I went straight to my car and sobbed the whole half-hour drive home.

I lost a lot of sleep that night. Partly because I felt so misjudged. Partly because I couldn't wrap my head around someone thinking it was heartless to choose life, but somehow it's "nice" to kill unborn babies. And partly because I lost a good friend. All because we couldn't comprehend each other's perspective.

My comprehension has since expanded.

A recent conversation has given me a greater understanding of the Pro-Choice position. I'm still adamantly Pro-Life, but I can finally grasp how someone can justify abortions and still be a "nice" person.

I will refer to my much younger friend as Kelly, although that isn't her real name. She is the peer of one of our older children. I didn't have much personal experience with Kelly, but I was aware of her background.

We have become more acquainted through Facebook. I have "watched" her work her way through college, get married, and start her career as a high school teacher. While we have dissimilar political views, we have a respectful relationship.

A few months ago, Kelly posted a Pro-Choice meme. Normally I just delete things I don't want on my News Feed, but a comment from a stranger caught my eye. It said something similar to:

"How can anyone with a heart not be Pro-Choice? And why would anyone want to control what another person does with her body? Why do they get so upset about it anyway? It's none of their business!"

I was reminded of the judgments placed on me by my former friend to which I had responded with tears rather than words. I was moved to respond. It went something like:

"I have a big heart (ask Kelly), but I am also Pro-Life. I'm choosing to answer your questions with an analogy, including some rhetorical questions. Pretend you see someone beating a dog to a bloody pulp. Would you turn your head the other way and pretend you didn't see it? Would you just say 'Hey, dude, that isn't cool'? Or would you actually try to stop the person and save the dog? The same passion that a caring person would have to save the dog is similar to the passion I feel about saving an unborn child."

I received a bombardment of rude comments and unsavory names but I just skimmed them. The one reply I did read was from Kelly, because I knew she wouldn't dismiss me so easily. After all, we had a history of respect for one another.

She responded with something like, "It isn't a valid comparison because a dog is a living, breathing creature that feels pain, but a fetus isn't."

My answer was, "I'm not comparing a dog to a human fetus, but the FEELING the situation invokes. A similar, fiery, bleeding-heart compassion to save the dog is what Pro-lifers feel every time we think of an abortion being performed. It isn't because we want to control what happens to the woman's body. It's because we want to save the innocent life of the body within. We are advocating for a human life whose voice can't yet be heard."

Kelly and I started a useful, respectful exchange. Not to persuade each other to change but to seek understanding of the other's point of view. We both put emotions aside and truly "listened" to one another. I wish I had somehow saved the conversation, but I didn't and it's probably floating around in the ethers for eternity.

I knew Kelly understood me when she said, "I guess if I believed that a fetus was really a human being, I would get upset, too."

I asked, "So you sincerely believe that a fetus isn't a human being?"

Her answer, "Yes, that's what I believe. Until it can live outside the womb, it's just a clump of cells. Having an abortion is no different than having a cyst removed."

Ahhhhh. I finally comprehended her standpoint. While from my perspective, abortion is snuffing out an innocent life, from Kelly's view, abortion is nothing more than a medical procedure.

We corresponded a little longer. The conversation was similar to the following.

I asked, "What about premature babies?"

"I don't believe in late-term abortions."

"So, when does a clump of cells become a viable human being?"

Kelly replied, "I don't know. No one does. Do you believe that life starts at conception? If so, what proof do you have?"

"I don't know exactly when life begins," I admitted. "But I would rather err on the side of life than risk causing the death of a unique human being."

Kelly gave her honest opinion. "I would rather destroy it before it is capable of knowing what's going on than risk having it born to someone who doesn't want it or overpopulating the world."

Did we agree? Absolutely not. Could we fathom each other's perspective? Yes. Are we still friends? Positively.

We thanked each other for the respectful, insightful conversation. It was a learning experience for both of us.

Airplane View

What does all this have to do with living your passion or dealing with dream-killers?

The ability to mentally step into someone else's shoes, see through their eyes, and, therefore, expand your awareness is like sprinkling fertilizer on the garden of your mind. It provides nourishment for your dream seed.

I call it an airplane view. Like an old-time crop duster, you can see the whole field instead of just your backyard. You can fertilize, prevent weeds, get rid of pests, whatever is needed. It helps you see more options.

By opening your mind and viewing things from different angles, you can more easily smooth out problems. Often you can even prevent them from happening at all. That's important as you prepare to present your dream to those you love the most.

I often ask myself, "Does this really matter in the long run?" Sometimes it does, sometimes it doesn't. But because I have viewed it from many angles, I can make rational choices instead of knee-jerk reactions.

Answering that question has greatly reduced my stress levels. It's probably added quality years to my life. I wish I had known all this 20 years ago, but I'm grateful to know it now.

So, if you don't do it already, how about giving it a try? Whatever your passion, tweak your perspective to include an occasional airplane view.

When building my MLM, I witnessed many people quit because they took their eye off the big picture and focused on a tiny part of it. They would look at a challenge and use it as an excuse not to move forward.

A frequent excuse I heard (and still do) is "I can't succeed because of my family. They take up so much time – there's Little League, ballet recitals, karate classes, etc. ...."

Others used (and still do) the same scenario to BUILD their businesses. "I will succeed because of my family. I will sacrifice some time with them now so we can have the time and money freedom to be together later – in Hawaii or Paris or New Zealand, etc. It will give us the freedom to provide the best possible education." Or better yet, they include their families in growing their businesses.

Obstacle? Or motivator. You decide.

One Final Story

On a sloppy, winter morning a year or two ago, I was driving to the airport in Buffalo, New York, to catch a flight to Dallas, Texas. It takes just under an hour on a clear day, but that particular morn, the roads were slushy and a light snow fell. I had allowed extra time but halfway into the trip, I realized I needed to go to the bathroom.

Have you ever had the experience when you don't want to take time to stop but you know if you don't, you'll soon be in agony? Ugh.

Instead of waiting to get to the airport and having to haul my luggage with me, I opted to visit a familiar supermarket chain whose restrooms were at the front of the building and, almost always, clean.

Parking as close as I could, I trudged through the dirty snow, and dashed to the empty women's restroom. There were two stalls - one handicapped, one regular. Soggy footsteps led to both. With the accumulation of snow outside, there was no way to keep the floor clean and dry no matter how often the staff checked.

It was western New York in January. That's life. I hurried as quickly as I could without sliding on the slippery spots. I automatically went to the regular stall but there was nowhere to hang my purse and coat. The hook had broken off.

I quickly darted to the handicapped stall, hung my things on the door hook, and did my duty. Still rushing, I put my coat on in the stall so I wouldn't have to set it on the wet floor to wash my hands. I slung my purse over my shoulder to head for the sink.

When I opened the door, I was surprised to see a woman, about my age, with a walker, glaring at me. If her eyes were guns, I'd have been riddled with bullets. I mean, she was livid!

"Oh, I'm sorry. I didn't know anyone was waiting," I offered, even though she couldn't have been waiting more than a minute. Probably less. She stood firm in her location by the sink, like a hawk ready to rip its prey. I had to move by her to get to the sink.

"How dare you!" She screeched. "How dare you use the handicapped bathroom! There's nothing wrong with you!"

That was just the opening of her tirade. While I proceeded to soap up my hands, she literally screamed at me, telling me what a horrible person I was to add suffering to a poor woman like her, that I had no heart, that I never thought about anyone but myself …".

A variety of emotions quickly surged through me: surprise, hurt, embarrassment, guilt, anger, pity … A few years earlier, I would have immediately reacted with a deluge of tears and melted to the floor to join the puddles of former snow. But tears were no longer my first response.

Several possible retorts zipped through my head as I continued to wash my hands, not looking at her. Good thing I don't curse.

Part of me wanted to say, "Look, Lady, if you need to use the bathroom so bad, why are you wasting your time yelling at me?"

A remnant of juvenility tempted me to face her with crossed-eyes, stick out my tongue, and walk out without saying another word.

I considered the option to yell back, using her own beginning words, "How dare you! How dare you judge me! You don't know me at all! And how do you know I don't have some kind of handicap you can't see? Maybe I have an ostomy bag or IBS, you don't know. You should look in the mirror when you call out those rude labels!"

And I admit, a sarcastic response swirled in my head, too. "Ya, know, sweetheart, I waited aaaall morning in this store just to get ahead of you in the handicapped stall. Just because I want to make you mad. That's what I live for - to make you miserable. And I succeeded. YAAAAY!!! (Insert evil laugh)"

The biggest part of me wanted to explain myself; about the hook on the door, that I rarely use a handicapped stall, and that I really am a nice person. But she was so riled up, that would take some time and there was no guarantee she would even listen to me. I didn't want to miss my flight.

So, I didn't say any of those things.

Instead, I tried to look at the situation from her perspective. Yes, she was choosing at that moment to have a chip on her shoulder and be nasty about it. But perhaps she was having a particularly rough morning. A hefty medical bill might be looming over her. Maybe her 18-year-old cocker spaniel was going to be put to sleep the next day. Was it possible that a side effect of her meds was irritability? Maybe from her point of view, the world was a mean, nasty, unfair place and the only way she knew how to react was to mirror it.

I had no idea her true standpoint, and I didn't have time to find out. And ultimately, it didn't matter. I was not responsible for her. I was responsible for me.

So, as I dried my hands, I looked her in the eyes with compassion. It startled her enough that she quit yapping.

"Ma'am, I'm truly sorry I inconvenienced you. It wasn't intentional, but at this point, there is nothing I can do but apologize. Please don't let it ruin your day."

With that, I left. Once back in my car, I prayed for her. No one venting such vile words and harboring such contempt and harsh judgment can have a perspective which allows for joy and expansion. She was keeping herself in a cage. I sincerely hoped she didn't hang on to the ill-will and didn't let it ruin her day.

I certainly didn't want it to ruin mine. So I prayed for me, too. With conscious effort, I let go of all the negative thoughts and feelings that had tumbled around inside of me during that brief but brutal encounter. I didn't want any dark bits lingering to stain my soul.

Can this help you navigate through emotions when confronted with a negative encounter? I sincerely hope so. Especially concerning interactions with your loved ones.

Next time you face a disagreement with your dream-killer, no matter how right you are from your perspective, try to understand where he is coming from. You don't have to agree with it, but look from his viewpoint so you can comprehend what he sees.

You can't change him, so change you.

Remember when I forgave my husband for his choices that I allowed to shatter my first dream? I couldn't do that until I had let myself view things from his standpoint. He didn't do anything TO me, he did it FOR himself. Perspective.

ACTION STEPS

For Your Passion:

- Find a friend that you know who has an opposing view on an issue related to your passion. Ask him if he would be willing to help you understand his point of view. Without judgment, listen and learn.

- Research websites, blogs, etc. to connect with people that are pursuing a similar passion to yours. Find out how they have handled challenges with people who didn't share their view.

- Choose one thing that you consider to be an obstacle to living your passion. Try looking at it from an airplane view. By tweaking your perception of it, can you flip the obstacle into a motivator?

- Write the following words on an index card (or something similar) and keep it where you can easily access it when a clash of perspectives come up: "In the long run, does this really matter?"

For Your Relationships:

- Now that you've tried out calmly addressing an opposing view with a friend, try it with your dream-killer. Don't choose a huge issue, just something small to test the waters. It doesn't have to be related to your passion. The purpose is to stretch the experience of exploring his viewpoint.

- This may seem silly if it isn't something you'd normally consider, but it can have a positive influence on the recipient. Write a note to your dream-killer that says something like the following (adapt it to be appropriate for both of you): "Even though we don't always look at things the same, I love you for who you really are." Put it where he will find it when you aren't together.

PART II

PRESENT

Outward Expression

In this section, you will be given tips to understand your dream-killer, to get inside his head to see what makes him tick. Through this awareness, you can develop a strategy to present your passion in a way that has the least risk of ridicule or rejection. By evaluating your encounter with your dream-killer, you can adapt your strategy if you choose to keep actively engaging your loved one. Or you may decide to become a true unipreneur and succeed solo in the same house. It's totally your choice. Either way, the tone is set to move forward and grow your dream!

CHAPTER 4

UNDERSTAND YOUR DREAM-KILLER

*"He who knows others is wise;
he who knows himself is enlightened."*

—Lao Tzu

Having birthed six children, I do not have credence in John Locke's "blank slate" theory which states that babies' brains are born completely void of any cognizance and that everything, that is EVERYTHING, must be taught.

Bologna.

Have you ever witnessed the first time a baby sees his fist? No one teaches him that it's part of his body and that he can eventually control its movement. The baby figures that out himself.

Each one of my munchkins was born with a distinct personality, specific likes and dislikes, a personal way of communicating, and a vast number of other unique qualities that were innate. Those were not learned traits. Sorry, Dr. Locke.

For example, one of our daughters was born a vegetarian. Literally. When she was old enough to start eating baby food, she would clamp her jaws shut whenever it had meat in it. Inexplicably, she knew the ingredients included bits of former living creatures, without even getting the spoon to her lips.

At the time of this writing, that daughter just turned 19 and has NEVER had even a tiny piece of meat in her mouth, let alone ingest it. She has absolutely, without question, never tasted meat.

That wasn't a learned behavior. I grew up in Texas, and we always had a side of beef in the freezer. My husband grew up in Oregon with all kinds of seafood, plus his parents butchered their own chickens and pigs. Meat was a daily habit for us, and we continued that tradition for over two decades. All five of our vegetarian daughter's siblings ate (well, mostly) whatever was put on the table. A deep aversion to meat somehow came with that tiny little person in the delivery room.

What does that mean?

That means you and I and our dream-killers all came into this world with lingerings from the pre-birth experience. We each have our own personalities and tendencies that can be strengthened or weakened through our environment, experiences, and choices.

The nature versus nurture debate? Personally, I think attention to BOTH is crucial to reaching our full potential.

"Know Thy Self, Know Thy Enemy"

The proverb above is attributed to the great Chinese military leader, Sun Tzu, in his writings, "The Art of War," although Tzu himself referred to them as words that were "widely said" at the time.

Whatever the origin, the concept is critical on so many levels other than on literal, physical battlefields. It can apply to the battles within one's head or heart. It can relate to the "wars" of words between oneself and others.

It can also apply to you and your dream-killer. I'm not saying your dream-killer is an enemy to YOU, but he is an enemy to your passion whether or not he views it that way.

Understanding how his brain ticks can give you an advantage on how to present your passion to him. Through studying personality types and how individuals most naturally give and receive communications, you will be more apt to express your longings in a way less likely to evoke ridicule or anger.

Ready to dive in?

I'm going to share a personal story now and there is part of it in which I will invite you to participate by imagining the instructions are being given to you personally. If you do so, you will have a better understanding of yourself and others, including your dream-killers. I'll give you a heads up before the exercise actually starts.

Near the beginning of my MLM career, I went to a 3-day conference with my upline daughter (not the vegetarian). We arrived early to the conference center and saw a couple hurriedly trying to set up a display table. The tall, athletic-looking man had a luggage cart full of heavy boxes, sealed with packing tape, that he was rushing to unload. The much smaller woman was scrambling to remove books and CDs from a box and arrange them on the table.

The man brusquely stopped unloading, and said something like, "No, no, not like that, like this ..." and proceeded to rearrange the books. The woman stepped back, observed for a moment, and then silently resumed her task. She looked up at him for approval. He nodded and went back to hefting the packages. He hadn't exactly been rude to her, but the atmosphere was tense.

I stepped up to the woman and said, "Would you like some help?"

"Oh, yes, that would be wonderful!" she replied, her demeanor dripping with gratitude.

"Thank you," said the man with a deep southern drawl. He offered a handshake. "I'm Robert, and this is my wife, April. That would be very helpful. These boxes were supposed to be on the same flight as us but there was a mix-up. We expected to be set up hours ago."

My daughter (who was helpful when asked but much too shy to initiate a conversation with strangers) and I joined in the work, making the task more manageable. We all worked tenaciously. Being very detail-oriented, my daughter also tweaked a few things without being told. The display looked great, all the boxes discreetly stowed under the table, and the luggage cart returned to the front desk shortly before conference-goers started to arrive.

"Wow," Robert commented, looking at the table. "It got done in time. And I've never seen our display look better. Thanks!"

His countenance had completely changed. A sparkle was in his eye, and he seemed bubbly with excitement. Before going into the conference room, we shook hands with Robert again. April opened her arms and hugged us freely, lavishing thanks. I felt like she was a long-time friend.

About an hour later, the main speaker was introduced. It was none other than our new friend at the display table, Dr. Robert A. Rohm, expert in human behavior. He was introduced as the author of several books, including "Positive Personality Profiles: D-I-S-C-over Personality Insights to Understand Yourself and Others!" and "Who Do You Think You Are Anyway?" He was also President of Personality Insights, Inc.

Dr. Rohm not only had fantastic information but presented it in a dynamic, engaging way that helped each of us internalize what we were learning. And entertaining? Oh. My. Goodness. My side hurt from laughing so hard. By the end of the weekend, my understanding of people had quadrupled. Maybe more. It literally changed my life.

He introduced us to the DISC personality styles, originated way back in 1928 by William Moulton Marston in his book titled *Normal People,* and the "DISC Personality Test" developed by Walter Cook in 1940. Dr. Rohm thoroughly understands their teachings and has expanded on them in ways that can help ANYONE willing to learn (and willing to apply what they learn!).

Dr. Rohm began with a practical exercise to help us discover for ourselves which were our prevalent personality styles. It was very effective.

An Exercise in Insight

I'm going to share the experience with you now, but please keep in mind that these are not Dr. Rohm's exact words. It's a re-creation taken from detailed notes I took over that conference weekend.

I now invite you to visualize yourself in the conference room with several hundred people. Picture Dr. Rohm up on the stage, his Georgia accent permeating his clear, energetic voice. Listen to the descriptions he gives and mentally follow his instructions.

He asked us to stand up and then said something like, "If you consider yourself to be outgoing ... that is you have a light inside and you love to shine it, come to the front of the room by me, up here by the stage. If you consider yourself to be more reserved, that is, you'd rather be quiet in the background than get up on stage, go to the back of the room."

We automatically separated ourselves.

In which direction did you go? Toward the stage? To the back?

Dr. Rohm continued, "If you just absolutely love people, I want you to go to the right of the room, my left. If you would much rather work on a project or complete a task than be with a group of people, I would like you to go to the left side of the room, my right."

Again, we naturally knew which direction to walk. We had separated ourselves into the four corners of the room.

In which corner are you now?

To the people at the left of the stage, he said in a very firm, deliberate voice, "You are the 'D' personalities. You are Dominant. You are all outgoing and task-oriented people. You have drive, ambition, and are not afraid to take charge. You are direct, to the point, and get things done with no nonsense. You are motivated by challenges and love to be in control. You'd much rather be the boss than have a boss." By that time, everyone in the "D" group was nodding their heads if not shouting "yes!" or "that's right!"

He turned to the group at the right of the stage and said in a faster-paced, excited voice, "You are the 'I' personalities. You are Inspiring. You are outgoing and people-oriented, and guess what? I'm one of you! We love recognition and approval. We're optimistic, persuasive, and creative. Because we're so friendly and enthusiastic, we have lots of friends and opportunities to influence others. We love to talk, swap stories, and have fun. Whoo-hoo! We're the life of the party!"

Pointing to the group in the far-right corner of the room, Dr. Rohm said in a very gentle, slower-paced voice, "And you, my friends. You are the "S" personalities. You are Supportive.

You are reserved but you are also people-oriented. You are the kindest, sweetest people on the planet Earth and you love to serve others. You love peace and harmony, security and assurance. You are steady, stable, dependable, and loyal. You love to be shown appreciation but not in grandiose ways. The words 'thank you' and even a simple smile can have a big positive impact on how you feel. You are the salt-of-the-earth."

He stiffened as he gestured to the far-left corner of the room and said with crisp, precise words, "And you are the "C" personalities. You are very Cautious. You are reserved and task-oriented. You want high quality answers to your myriad of questions. You love efficiency, order, precision, and excellence. You have high standards and expect them of others. You are conscientious, analytical, systematic, and you are able to solve problems, some of which the rest of us don't even know exist yet. You are masters at figuring out details and solutions."

It was uncanny how accurately he described the members of each group.

How about yours? Did Dr. Rohm depict some of your personality traits? I know he did mine.

He went further to say we each also have a secondary personality that we often fall back on when conditions aren't exactly how we'd choose.

We weren't asked to move again, but we were asked to point to another corner of the room to a different personality type with which we identified.

It was amazing. As if on cue, literally half of each of the four groups pointed to the group on their direct left while the other half pointed to the group on their direct right. There may have been one or two people who pointed to the corner opposite of them.

One more surprise came.

Dr. Rohm asked if there were any married couples in the room. Probably 100 people raised their hands. Then Dr. Rohm said, "Point to your spouse."

Almost all (not quite) pointed to the opposite corner. If my husband had been there, that's where he would have been. I guess opposites DO attract! It taught me that not only does my hubby have different experiences and perspectives than me, his personality is wired differently, too.

Hmm. That knowledge held a lot of possibilities for positive change.

Dr. Rohm taught many more things that weekend, way too much to share here, but I want to return to the account of first meeting Robert and April as they scurried to set up their display table. After attaining more awareness of the personality types, I was able to view that first encounter differently.

Robert, an "I", was stressed and had slipped into his secondary personality style, "D", in order to get the job done quickly. He hadn't been rude to his wife, he was merely taking charge of the unexpected situation to remedy it. Had he remained in "I", he may have been too distracted to get anything accomplished.

Now I don't know April's true personality style, but as that display table was being put together, she was a solid "S". Sweet as honey, complying with orders in silence, avoiding confrontation.

I was also in "S" mode, although my "I" did come out as I joked to lighten up the initial tension.

My daughter, a "C", followed me into the "S" style in order to serve the Rohms. However, her "C" came out as she tweaked the arrangement of books and CDs to give the display a very organized, polished look.

Internalizing this information has helped me tremendously in the past decade. Relationships with my peers, business associates, and family members (especially the dream-killers) have vastly improved.

By understanding your own personality style AND that of your dream-killer, you will have insight on how and why he responds certain ways. My hope is that this new awareness will help you develop a plan to share your dream seed that will evoke the best possible scenario. And if there is a conflict, it will help you deal with it in a more positive way.

That Thing Called Love

Through the personal development resources of my MLM company, I was introduced to the book *"The Five Love Languages"* by Gary Chapman. It was another eye-opener. It not only helped me understand my husband better, but myself and our children as well. Mr. Chapman has since written numerous books on subjects pertaining to relationships.

I have not yet had the pleasure of meeting Gary Chapman, but I'm very grateful for his teachings. I believe they can help you, too!

The premise is that there are five basic ways (or "languages") we humans use to express and feel love. Each one of us has one or two dominant love languages with which we communicate - both giving and receiving. If we understand our own language and that of the person we are trying to connect with, we are more likely to have a positive interaction.

Again, it's a matter of awareness. If we are conscious of the languages, we can adjust our communications accordingly. It must also be noted that there are dialects within those five languages, depending on culture, personal experience, attitude, perspective, personality, etc. But knowing the basic five can help tremendously.

I will briefly describe the five love languages in no particular order.

Words of Affirmation - Verbal compliments, praise, and appreciation speak louder than actions, especially if they are offered unexpectedly. Straightforwardness is best. Don't beat around the bush, just say it.

Hearing the words are even more powerful when the reasons behind them are also shared. For example, "I appreciate you" is awesome to hear, but "I appreciate you because of the way you know how to fix things" is even better.

Besides the spoken word, written words can be powerful, too. A little note of praise taped to the dashboard of his car, "You're SO handsome!" written in lipstick on the bathroom mirror, a Post-It note with "I'm grateful you are in my life" penned inside a red heart can all spark joy in his (and your) life.

When my husband and I were first engaged, we took a college "marriage class" together. The teacher said something like, "don't be afraid to write 'I love you' in the butter so your spouse will see it unexpectedly." We chuckled at the time but over the years, there have been several occasions when one of us found those three words carved into a stick or tub of margarine. It melted more than just the butter.

Quality Time - Time is a precious and nonrenewable commodity. In its purest form, this love language requires undivided attention with no distractions. It means sharing quality conversations and activities.

In this day of personal electronics, people who naturally crave quality time, suffer. Sitting at the same table with someone staring at his phone just doesn't cut it. Neither does going on a walk together, one wearing earbuds, listening to music. It requires mutual interaction.

I'll admit it came as a surprise to me when "quality time" topped the list of my husband's love languages. Remember him wanting me to ride bikes with him? It wasn't because he wants me to ride a bike. It's because he wants me to spend time with him, sharing in an activity he absolutely loves. He was telling me he loves me.

It used to bug me when I had to go grocery shopping and Hubby would tag along. The task took at least twice as long, and we always ended up with way more in the cart than was on my list. I knew he hated shopping, so I couldn't understand why he'd want to go.

Then it dawned on me. He didn't want to go grocery shopping. He just wanted to spend time with me. In truth, it was a big compliment. We lived out in the country, so a trip to the store meant at least a half hour in the car together. That's an opportunity for some quality conversation.

Now when I go shopping, I usually invite him along unless I'm in a rush. And I allow a lot more time. We not only enjoy the ride together, but also the leisurely strolls down the aisles looking at all kinds of stuff we don't need. Although it seems a bit silly from my original standpoint, now I look at it as going on a date. It works for us.

Physical Touch - This may be intimate, romantic touch but that definitely isn't the only kind. Hugs and kisses, hand-holding, and pats on the back are all fuel for fulfillment. Even small touches on his arm or face, perhaps stroking his hair, are all ways to show love, concern, and caring. It's human nature (with the exception of some people with medical or psychological issues) for physical touch to foster a sense of security and belonging.

I grew up in a very touchy-feely family. We hugged frequently, scratched each other's backs, and had tickle fights. It wasn't uncommon to be on the couch and have a sibling's legs across my lap. As the youngest, I remember being carried piggy-back or on my brother's shoulders. I continued that with our six children even though my husband is NOT naturally touchy-feely. It's an effort for him.

If physical touch isn't your first love language, but it is your dream-killer's, make a conscious effort to provide more. Next time you see him sitting in a kitchen chair, try massaging his shoulders. Even touching his back or running your fingers down his arm as you pass by can provide positive feelings.

Watching TV together? Sit close with your legs touching. Intertwine your arm with his and snuggle up. Form a habit of making physical contact whenever you are both in the room. No matter how small the touch, it will add up to good feelings.

Acts of Service - To help lessen workloads and ease burdensome responsibilities is what triggers the love in this language.

"Here, honey, let me mow the grass this time" or "I'll go pick up the kids so you don't have to" are living statements of devotion and appreciation.

Frankly, this is my hot button in both giving and receiving. I have countless opportunities to show love for my family by filling their needs, but additional acts of service - going above and beyond the duties of parenthood - gives me great joy. So does volunteer work in my church and community. I love to ease burdens, relieve suffering, and "go the extra mile."

Having said that, it can eventually feel burdensome when my acts of service aren't appreciated or reciprocated. When my husband, children, or friends step in to work alongside me (without being asked) or even ease some of my responsibilities, it means the world to me. It raises my spirits and helps me feel loved.

Receiving Gifts - For this language, a "gift" is a visual representation of love and consideration. It's usually an actual, tangible item or event but it can also include gestures. It can be extravagant like a new car or a cruise, or it can be simple like a box of Girl Scout cookies or tickets to a movie. The important thing is to put thought into it and give him something HE would like. You wouldn't want to give a fur coat to an animal rights activist!

Another good thing about giving gifts is that it can cover more than one love language. For example, give him a paid weekend trip to a beach resort. Besides the gift itself, you will also provide the opportunity for quality time together and physical touch. You can shower him with words of affirmation while providing the service of slathering sunscreen on his back. Voila! All five love languages were communicated! Be creative. Have fun.

Even though giving gifts was the lowest on my list (it only received a score of 1 in contrast to my first which had 12), I still appreciate a considerate gift. For me, I choose to view a thoughtful gift as an act of service. The item or gesture is of great worth because of what it represents, not necessarily the gift itself.

Although I admit, when my husband slips a Snickers candy bar into my computer bag, I thoroughly enjoy the thought AND the gift. I feel loved. Especially if it's a Snickers with almonds.

Last Note

Now you should have at least a basic understanding of the five Love Languages. But there is one more thing to consider: It's just as important to know what your love languages ARE NOT.

For example, my No. 1 language by far is Acts of Service. It's my husband's last. For years, I would do things for him as an expression of love but he would react with indifference or, at best, a simple "oh, thanks." It hurt me. I felt rejected and insignificant.

So, what did I do? I tried harder by doing MORE acts of service. All I got was more of the same. Finally, I quit doing the "extras" and lavished acts of service on those who appreciated it.

On the flip side, since it's Hubby's least valuable language, he didn't do many acts of service for me unless I asked him. In my brain, that didn't really count. Therefore, it wasn't many years before I only asked him for help if I absolutely couldn't do something myself, like lift heavy objects or reach a high shelf. It left me unfulfilled because I thought he didn't really love me.

Now, however, because I am aware of our primary love languages, I don't take his lack of service as a slight. I don't take it personally anymore. I accept that it just isn't his love language. And that's okay.

One more thing. Even though each of us has primary and secondary personality styles and love languages, we all have the capacity to develop strengths in each style and language. The more balanced we are, the better.

For example, a natural "I/S" like me has developed skills in the "D" style when leading my children or volunteers. Same with "C" traits. I couldn't keep track of finances or run my businesses if I stayed in "I" or "S" all the time. And I have developed all five love languages because in a family of eight, I need to be fluent in each one to provide the best possible atmosphere at home.

Am I perfect at it? Heck no! But the point is, I keep trying. And little by little, I get better at it. You can, too.

So what's your primary love language? What's your dream-killer's? Being aware of your love language and personality style, as well as his, can help you successfully navigate through this presentation stage of living your passion.

Your dream seed has now been planted in fertile soil and taken root. Do the Action Steps to keep it nourished and protected. It's almost time to bring your healthy little seedling into the light!

ACTION STEPS

For Your Passion:

- Go to www.UnipreneurBook.com to find out how to learn more about personality styles. You will also find links to the following Action Steps.

- Choose either the DISC Personality Profile or the 16 Personalities test and take the FREE online assessment. You can also do both, if you choose. Study the results.

- Take the Five Love Language Test and be enlightened by the results.

- Apply the information you have learned about personality styles and love languages to your relationships with family, friends, and co-workers. Try to decipher their actions (and reactions) in order to understand them better. This builds a better YOU, which, in turn, strengthens your position to move forward with your passion.

For Your Relationships:

- Now that you've taken the assessment for either DISC Personality Profile or the 16 Personalities test, share what you've learned with your dream-killer. Try your best to get him to take the free assessment, too. If he won't, then make a hard copy of the test and sporadically ask him the questions. Record his answers and submit them when you get them all. Only guess his answers as a last resort because the results will be less accurate.

- Since you've taken the Five Love Language Test, get your dream-killer to do the same. To coax him, if needed, tell him that by discovering his best love languages, you can better fill his needs. Or bribe him. I got my hubby to take it by asking him on our anniversary. Whatever works. If he absolutely will not take the test, then experiment by communicating with him using one love language at a time and observe which ones bring the greatest response.

CHAPTER 5

DECLARE YOUR PASSION

"It's so hard to communicate because there are so many moving parts. There's presentation and there's interpretation and they're so dependent on each other it makes things very difficult."

—Garth Stein

I don't know the exact context in which fellow writer and film producer, Garth Stein, penned the statement above, but I do understand it. It can, indeed, be hard to communicate in a way that all parties fully understand one another. However, when dealing with your in-house dream-killer, you have two big factors in your favor.

First, since you choose to have the person remain in your life, you obviously have high incentive for clear communication. Otherwise, you already would have chosen your passion over your partner. You'd be long-gone. I believe if you and your dream-killer truly love each other and want to remain together while you follow your dream, you can. I'm not saying it will be easy, but with desire and determination, you can succeed with both.

Second, you should now have more insight into how both you and your loved one are wired. Hopefully, you've followed the Action Steps and viewed things through your dream-killer's eyes. You understand the best way to communicate with him. If you share the same love language, awesome! If not, that's okay, too. It just may take a little more concentration. But whatever, you're willing to focus on using HIS love language and addressing HIS personality style, even if those aren't what come most naturally to you.

Avoid My Blunders

Remember my experience of telling Hubby about the MLM? I was in my high "I" with excitement which did NOT connect with his high "C" or strong "D" in the least. And I'm sure I didn't speak his love language. I had no clue of such things back then. My passion presentation didn't go well. Not well at all.

If I could do it over, I would prepare for the moment by spending some quality time together doing something HE enjoys. Like building a campfire in the backyard and roasting hot dogs (Yuck! Hot dogs are gross!). Or hiking one of the trails at the nearby Wildlife Refuge (Yay! I like that one, too!). I believe such "together time" would put him in the most receptive mood possible.

I would further prep him by making a pumpkin pie (his favorite) and letting him know it's just for him. He doesn't have to share it. And maybe I would also give him his own container of whipped topping with his name on it; he won't have to share that, either.

Those may seem like little things, but when you live in a house with a lot of kids, a pumpkin pie lasts about two minutes. And if you could find a container of whipped topping that wasn't completely empty, you might find scooped-out fingerprints in it. Or crumbs. Or worse. So, believe me, that would be a very considerate gift for my hubby, which would be a communication in another of his strong love languages.

What would prime your dream-killer? What would give him a smile, set him at ease, and open his heart?

Get in the Zone

Speaking of being at ease and having an open heart, those are things that YOU will need to have, too. Just like with an athlete, getting in the zone doesn't happen by accident. The more prepared you are, the better. I learned the hard way that a dream seed is not something to share on the fly.

I suggest you block out at least a couple of hours for your passion presentation, a time that is convenient for both of you when you won't be rushed. Not your lunch hour from work. Not between appointments. Not just before your daughter's soccer game.

This is a big deal, so plan it accordingly. It's much better to allow extra time than to have too little. You don't want to have to dash out with an unfinished conversation. Not one that is THIS important!

Determine a comfortable place where you won't be interrupted. Ideally, that would be in your place of residence so you won't have a devoted waitress, noisy traffic, or random people invading your space.

However, homes can be distracting, too. Make sure the kiddos aren't home, your pets are fed, the TV is off, etc., so that you can truly focus on each other. And have all electronic devices turned off. Not just silenced, OFF. It's amazing what a simple buzz can do to divert attention.

There is one more important consideration when preparing to share your dream. This may seem like back-tracking a little, but once you have the place and time set for you passion presentation, also allow for a period of solitude immediately before it's scheduled to begin. This is a vital time for mental preparation; it's when you truly get in the zone.

This is a personal, individualized observance. Whatever you do to step into that state, designate time for it.

In my case, there would be either silence or soft music. Or perhaps the barely audible sounds of a babbling brook or drizzling rain. Deep, conscious breaths would cleanse away anxiety and fear. In the attitude of prayer and meditation, I would express gratitude until I truly felt it with every fiber of my being. I would ask for strength and guidance.

Then would come a very crucial part of my practice: I would be still and listen. Remembering that I am an infinite being in a finite body, I would connect with God and hear His voice in my heart. I would know exactly what to say to my dream-killer. And I would have the demeanor to express it in a way that is most likely to be well-received.

That may seem crazy if you haven't experienced something like what I just shared, but if you have, you know how awesome it is. Nothing (no-thing) that is good and expansive is impossible if God is supporting you. Do all you can, and He will take up the slack.

The bottom line? Allow enough time to get in the zone, whatever that looks like to YOU.

Again, if I could have a re-do with sharing my MLM, I would preface my passion presentation with something like, "I have something to share with you. It means a lot to me and I've decided to pursue it. I have no idea what you'll think about it but I love you, I know you love me, too, and I would appreciate if you would hear me out before judging it."

Since Hubby is a high "C," I would also have a list of all the benefits of the company, my goals, and how I planned to achieve them. I would keep my emotions under control and speak with logic.

That's what I did with the real estate investment company. He still didn't jump up and down about it, but he accepted that I was going to do it with or without his support. Even though his idea of real estate investing is buying vacant land and sitting on it for 30 years and mine is to build passive income on a continuing basis NOW, he chose not to fight me on it. No name calling, no ridicule, just a grumpy face. And I can deal with that. I have enough smiles for the both of us.

As a result, the real estate investments started providing income much faster than it took me to build my MLM business. It isn't because the opportunity was better, but I was better. I started on a higher plane. Through the MLM process, I not only learned business skills and personal development, but I had more self-confidence and awareness. I was an improved version of ME.

So how about you? Hopefully, you've had some personal growth since you started reading this book. You've expanded your mind and your people skills. It's YOUR turn to step forward and share your dream.

On Your Mark, Get Set ...

Now that you understand his personality type, present your passion in a way that is most acceptable to HIM. I'm going to reemphasize: That may mean doing the total opposite of what YOUR personality style would naturally do.

I'll give some examples:

- If he is a high "D," speak to him in a straightforward, empowered voice with direct eye contact. I don't mean challenge him (remember, he loves to be in control) but be a cohort. Stroke his ego first. You could prep him with, "I love the powerful way you take charge and make things happen. I have something important to me that I want to share. With your support, I know this will be big ..."

- If he is a high "I," you could say something like, "Guess what? I have a HUGE idea. It's going to be so much fun, and I want you right there with me!" Use an excited tone of voice, hand gestures, and lots of body language. Charge up the energy and let it crackle. Hopefully, your enthusiasm will rub off on him, and he'll catch the same vision.

- If he is a high "S," keep in mind that safety and security are at the top of his list of wants. Change is not easy for him, especially if it is drastic or unexpected. He doesn't like his boat rocked, so nudge it gently. Instead of telling him all at once, you might consider giving it to him piecemeal and letting him get used to it a little at a time. Like gradually walking into a swimming pool instead of diving in.

- If he is a high "C," consider having a list of bullet points in your hand as you speak. Remember that because he focuses on details so much, he has a hard time seeing the big picture. He may be quick to see flaws and jump on them. However, he also wants to avoid conflict, which is a plus for you. With clear enunciation, you could start with, "I know you love having all the details in front of you, and I will do my best with that, but I have a burning passion that I want to share with you. I'd really love for you to help me figure it all out." Even if he doesn't grasp your vision, he may be willing to help you out since he loves you (and he loves solving problems).

Get the drift?

Ding! The Buzzer Just Sounded ...

The time has come to share your passion. The dream seed has been planted and is a healthy little sprout. You've nurtured it, sheltered it, and the moment has arrived to set it in full sunlight.

Please keep in mind, however, that your dream-killer has free agency to think and act as he chooses. While you may be so excited about your dream that your eye twitches, your partner may not. Respect that. Don't try to talk him into believing as you do, just share. If he asks questions and sincerely wants to know more - great! If not, don't try to force it. Again, just share.

Whatever happens, don't forget what you have already learned — that while your vision is clear to you, it may not be to your loved one. Your attitude is a choice and so is your partner's. You may have different viewpoints now but that doesn't mean it can't change.

Stay strong but loving and your perspectives just might eventually align. You can do this!

PostScript

Obviously, you can't sit down with your dream-killer, have your passion presentation, and read this book all at the same time. So before you take the last "For Your Passion" Action Step, there is one more issue to be addressed.

Balance.

Over the years, I have found that the most peaceful times in my life happen when there is balance - spiritually, mentally, and physically. For example, I serve others but I also see that my own needs are met. My days include time with family, business associates, church friends, and by myself. My food choices include a variety from all the food groups.

Exercise? Yes! That includes something in all three of the recommended areas: endurance, strength, and flexibility. (And by the way, my husband fit me with a bicycle, and I have started short rides with him - that actually gives me some exercise in all three areas, especially endurance. Yay!)

In other words, there is equilibrium. Those time periods are wonderful. They rejuvenate me, fill my well, so to speak. I find inner peace and tranquility. However, sooner or later, I find myself restless and discontent. Balance is insufficient. My spirit seeks more.

Have you ever felt that way?

I used to think it was selfish to be dissatisfied with the status quo. After all, I have my basic needs met, I live in a relatively safe environment, and I have freedoms that many people in the world do not. Aren't I being ungrateful if I want more?

No! I've delightfully discovered that it is neither selfishness nor a lack of gratitude that encourages me to reach higher, learn new things, seek new experiences, develop new skills, and pursue my passion. I get discontent because I'm not the best ME yet.

Frankly, I think that's why there are so many grumpy people in developed countries. Individuals languish because they are stagnant. Their spirit strives to be bigger, better, more expansive, more aware - to live their passion and offer their unique gifts to the world. But they don't. For whatever reason, they choose to stick their dream seed in a drawer, in a closet, on a shelf. Therefore, nothing changes. They stay in the rut; they stay average.

Not me. I no longer settle for mediocrity.

I don't think you do, either. That's why your eyes are on this page. You know you have more to offer the world, too.

So, what does all this mean?

Expect your life to get temporarily out of balance as you pursue your passion. Look at any "successful" person and you'll see that their time, effort, resources were directed in one area as they built their business, trained for their sport, apprenticed for their particular field, whatever. That doesn't mean complete abandonment of other areas of life, but a stripping of the unnecessary.

Broad, la-dee-da vision doesn't get big results. Laser focus can cut through steel. But the laser doesn't stay turned on continually. There are periods of down-time to recharge. Balance, then focused imbalance. It's an upward spiral.

For example, creating this book. I made the conscious choice to block time to write, which means I had to block out other activities from creeping onto my calendar. That isn't easy for me. Remember, I am a high "I". I love to be with people and have fun. My "S" is also high (barely below the "I") so I love to serve others. It's VERY hard for me to say no when asked to do anything positive.

I've had to prioritize. Have I declined social gatherings that I would have loved to attend? Yep. Have I said no to service projects that don't require my particular expertise? Absolutely. Have I neglected my family's needs? Nope. Have I said no to some of their wants? Much to their chagrin at times, yes.

I still teach the 6-year-olds at church and direct the congregational music, but I don't volunteer for extras at this time. That is, unless moved upon by a higher power to do so. That's a different story. I'm much more discretionary with my time and effort.

With my real estate investment business, I also had to make some hard choices. I'm currently not seeking any new properties and have delegated some of the responsibilities that I would normally do myself. So, while the business itself isn't growing, it's still maintaining a positive cash flow that should continue while I concentrate on this book.

And my MLM?

Hmm. I'll admit, I slipped a bit on that one. I hadn't been going to many of the functions I had previously attended on a regular basis. I also hadn't been as accessible to my downline. Therefore, the business hadn't grown as in times past because I hadn't focused my efforts there. Totally my fault.

However, I have awesome upline, Cheryl and Dave, that noticed. Cheryl called to set up a meeting and I chose to fit it in. They asked point blank what was going on. I expressed my passion for writing "Unipreneur" that I felt God had put it in my heart to share.

"There are people out there who need the message so they don't have to spend 10+ years figuring it out themselves. It's time to write the book now. Not later. NOW."

Dave said something like, "Wow, you should see how you lit up when you started talking about this book. Your eyes sparkle. You glow. It's like bells and whistles going off."

Cheryl locked eyes with me and said quietly, "You've thought a lot about this, haven't you?"

"Yes."

After only a moment's pause she asked, "What can we do to help?"

I replied immediately, "Take care of my people so I can concentrate on the manuscript."

She replied simply, "You got it!" And she has been true to her word.

I gave her my self-imposed deadline to have the manuscript finished, and she agreed to take over my business responsibilities until that time. Since that meeting, I did the bare minimum to keep my personal business from shrinking while Cheryl and Dave helped my downline to build their organizations. Kudos to my dedicated upline! They rock.

Although there is much more to publishing a book than putting words on paper, a completed manuscript is a major achievement. Cheryl recognized that. She scheduled a celebration party with our business associates around the time of my deadline. I think part of the reason was to spur me on to completion. It worked. We are, after all, dream-builders, not dream-killers.

My take-away for you?

Appreciate balance in your life, enjoy the experience when it happens, but don't expect to constantly live there. Perhaps consider it a vacation spot rather than a residency. Be aware that once you declare your passion, life will get a little (okay, more than just a little) unbalanced as you laser-focus on accomplishing it. Amazing things happen when you step outside your comfortable little box.

ACTION STEPS

For Your Passion:

- Review Chapters 2 and 3 about attitude and perspective. Refresh your resolve to have the best possible mental outlook when you share your dream seed with your loved one. Also, review Chapter 4 and the results of your online personality test and 5 Love Language test. If you haven't already determined your dream-killer's personality style and love language, do it now.

- Plan the actual date, time, and place for your passion presentation to your loved one.

- Practice getting "in the zone" to help ease any anxiety you may feel in anticipation of presenting your dream seed.

- Have your passion presentation. Declare your dream!

NOTE TO READER: I realize this is a HUGE step. If you're still unsure how to approach your dream-killer, please feel free to finish the rest of the book and come back to this Action Step. After all, this is the act that will designate you as a true Unipreneur. Three cheers for YOU!

For Your Relationships:

- In the days previous to your passion presentation, do five "extra" things for your dream-killer in his two best love languages to let him know you truly care about him.

- Choose to continue to love your dream-killer regardless of how he responds to your presentation. It's called unconditional love. And it's beautiful.

CHAPTER 6

EVALUATE YOUR ENCOUNTER

"As a principle-centered person, you try to stand apart from the emotion of the situation and from other factors that would act on you, and evaluate the options."

—Stephen R. Covey

Sometimes sharing your dream is like fly fishing. You cast out your vision to those you love the most. It's possible they'll immediately get hooked. More often, you have to reel in the line and try again. And again. And again. Until finally, one day you share your dream and they "get it."

If your loved one ended up getting totally hooked on your passion and has designated himself as your biggest fan, KUDOS! You don't have to be a unipreneur. However, you can still gain valuable information and tools from the rest of this book, whatever your circumstances. And I'm 99.99

percent sure you know someone who is in a unipreneur situation who could use your support.

If it didn't go well, pull back and keep your dream to yourself again, continue to nurture and shelter it. Take a deep breath and regroup. Don't give up. This process can be repeated over and over again. Someday it may work. Or it may not. But either way, you have put your stake in the ground.

Congratulations! You are officially a unipreneur.

Time for Assessment

You've reached an important juncture. Before bolting forward, step back to evaluate your encounter. Sincerely try to view it from your loved one's perspective. What you see will impact decisions you'll soon have to make.

Unless your dream-killer is actually cruel and/or dangerous (in which case, I strongly suggest you rethink your decision to stay in the relationship), it's likely that his negative response was based on one of three things: inconsideration, misunderstanding, or fear. These can overlap.

For example, when my hubby lost his faith and emotionally abandoned our family, it was based on inconsideration. He didn't intentionally kill my dream or confuse the children. Truth was, he didn't think of us at all. He didn't pause to reflect on how it would affect us as individuals or as a family, he was focused solely on himself. Long-term consequences never entered his mind. In other words, inconsideration.

As for my MLM? I think Hubby's reaction was based on misunderstanding and subconscious fear, although it took me years to realize it. At the time, I just thought he was being mean. More on that later.

Let's look at some possible responses. I'll start with some of the nicer ones. Did your dream-killer say anything similar to these?

- I just want you to be safe.
- It would be so much work for you.
- You're too busy as it is.
- Things are good enough now.
- Be content with the way things are.
- I don't want to see you disappointed.
- Why risk failure?

These are just a few examples of what your loved one might have said because he loves you. He wants to protect you. However genuine his concerns might be, he doesn't understand how deep your passion, how precious your gift, how vibrant your dream seed. He doesn't yet understand that you are willing to put in the work and take the risks.

The challenge is, he loves you and wants you to be safe. The advantage is, he loves you and wants you to be happy. The key phrase? He loves you. That means there is still opportunity for him to see how much your dream means to you. You can continue progressing as a unipreneur, showing him that it's a true passion, not just a passing fancy.

Some dream-killer responses are knee-jerk reactions stemming from a scarcity mindset. If he truly thinks there isn't enough for everyone, then he might say to you:

- If you want more, that means someone will have less. Do you really want to be that selfish?

- We're doing fine. If you change it, we might lose everything.

- There isn't enough money to get you started, let alone sustain it.

- That'll put us into debt that we can never pay off.

- We've already got our piece of the pie. There's no more to go around.

- I don't want to risk going without.

Again, if he really believes those things, then your dream seed is a threat to his world. Acknowledge his mindset but don't give in to it. After all, a mindset is just that - a set mind. We've already established that a closed mind does not allow for expansion and growth.

If you know your dream-killer's history (his story), then you may already understand past or present circumstances that have catered to his scarcity belief.

Was he raised in a family that constantly struggled with finances? Has there been deep disappointment over a failed attempt to follow a dream? Was there a time when he didn't have enough of something basic like food, shelter, clothing, love, or safety? Even a short but intense period of lack can have deep impact.

For example, both my parents were born in the 1920s, meaning they grew up during the Great Depression. It affected them both in very different ways.

My mother, Susanne, lived with her five siblings on a farm in Oklahoma. While they didn't have many material "things" and had to work relentlessly, there was always plenty of food - even enough to share with less fortunate community members. Mom continued the tradition of hard work, generosity, and compassion for others throughout her entire life.

However, my father, Richard, and his two younger sisters nearly starved. His family lived in various cities in Ohio, their father continually struggling to find work to support them. As soon as my dad was old enough, he also found jobs to help put food on the table but there was rarely enough.

I remember Dad trying to describe how it felt to be a young teenage boy, ravenous but with nothing to satisfy his aching belly. There were days when all he had to eat was one small potato.

Having three sons of my own, I can only imagine how they could've managed with so little food. In their teen years, it was not uncommon for our family to go through three loaves of bread and two gallons of milk a day. One potato a person? It pains me to even think of it.

Dad related how sometimes his stomach hurt so badly at night that he couldn't sleep. He'd sneak outside and walk for hours until the exhaustion was greater than the hunger. Of course, I'm sure burning up those calories didn't help, but he was just doing what he could to survive the moment.

It affected his psyche. He developed a fear of scarcity that he never quite overcame in his 93 years on this earth.

He was a decorated fighter pilot in World War II, a pilot for a major commercial airline for 36 years, a two-term mayor, successful investor, and had many other titles I could share. But in spite of his obvious success in life, he had a gnawing fear deep in his gut that somehow he would be left destitute. As a result, he counted pennies, spread his earnings among many bank accounts, and hid stashes of cash. It literally pained him to spend money.

My siblings and I grew up modestly. That isn't a complaint. I had a wonderful childhood, and we never knew lack. But it did come as a shock to me in high school when I discovered Dad brought in a lot of money. And I'm grateful that because of his great work ethic, smart investment choices, and frugality, he was well cared for during the long illness that ultimately took his life. Also thanks to him, my mother has means to continue a comfortable lifestyle for the remainder of her years.

Yet, I feel Dad missed out by not experiencing the joy of generosity that is such a big part of my mother's character. He donated regularly to his church and several charities, but it wasn't easy for him. It was out of duty and good citizenship, not from natural generosity. I fully understand his viewpoint but wish he had changed it to one of abundance. I don't think he knew he could.

So, what about your dream-killer?

Remember Chapter 3 on perspective? If you can view your passion through your dream-killer's eyes, you may be able to initiate some cracks in his scarcity mindset.

If not, perhaps at some point you could gently but directly ask him why he feels that way. Listen with the purpose to understand him, not to change his mind. Sometimes voicing the reasons for a belief helps the person question and expand his mode of thinking.

Another mindset of a dream-killer might be that rich, successful, powerful people must have done something illegal or immoral to get where they are. This was a belief of my hubby. He has said more than one of the following statements.

- No one succeeds unless he's bought.
- You have to sell your soul to become rich or famous.
- You can't be a good person and wealthy at the same time.
- It's dog eat dog to get to the top.
- Money is the root of all evil, so if your passion also brings in big dough, you'll be bad.
- No one can be successful without giving up his integrity.

Is it possible your dream-killer fears if he has wealth, fame, success, or power that he will abuse it or misuse it? If so, might he also fear what YOU would do with those assets?

Each of the dream-killer statements carry a grain of truth. Are there famous, affluent people who crushed others to gain their position? Have individuals been immoral, unethical, or otherwise sold out in exchange for their success?

Unfortunately, yes. Many of them. But that doesn't mean the statements are absolute. In each case, it was a matter of personal choice. You don't have to exchange moral or ethical values for success.

Quite the opposite. I encourage you to move upward by becoming a better YOU in all areas of your life. Pursue your passion by expanded awareness and appropriate action and your success will be sweet, both for you and for others.

I realize that your passion may or may not include financial freedom. And I'm also aware that having money does not necessarily make you successful. There are countless examples of wealthy people who are miserable failures in other areas of their lives, such as with relationships or health.

However, let me say that access to money opens doors to options that may be closed to you without it.

So, about this "money is the root of all evil" statement - that's a misquote. My hubby threw that one at me in one of his early rants against my MLM. I looked it up to prove the inaccuracy.

It comes from the Bible (King James Version) in 1 Timothy 6:10, which actually says "The LOVE of money is the root of all evil ..." That's only a two-word difference but it changes the meaning.

Money is just a tool, a medium of exchange. It's a "thing" which can't be virtuous or evil. Like a rock. Or a shovel. They can all be used for good or ill, but the objects themselves are morally neutral.

It's the attitude about money that can be evil. Has the love of money caused pain, disillusionment, murder, even wars? Absolutely! But not the money itself.

Ask yourself these questions:

- Hasn't the use of money also provided comfort, relief, the sustenance for life itself?
- Can a person without food provide it for another?
- Will a person who's broke be able to provide for his family's basic needs?
- Can he nurture the dream seeds in his heart?
- What about the God-given gifts each of us have; can we develop those when we are in survival mode?

Hopefully, you get my point.

I suggest that if your dream-killer is at least a little bit open to a calm exchange of ideas with you, set a time for an open discussion. Ask leading questions to discover the basis for his belief that a "good" person can't be more than moderately successful.

For example:

- Was he taught this by an authority figure such as a parent, teacher, or religious leader?
- Does he have personal experience with someone who traded their honor or virtue to get gain?
- Has he tried to succeed in a business venture that failed and needed an excuse to not try again?

Exploring the basis for his belief can bring understanding. That, in turn, can help you decide your next move as a unipreneur.

Silent Fears

Your dream-killer may also have fears that he won't express out loud. Is it possible he might be thinking any of the following?

- What if you become more successful than I am?
- What if you make more money than I do?
- If you succeed, you might leave me.
- Your passion will become more important to you than I am.
- You won't need me anymore.
- I'll be neglected.
- If you fail, we'll both look stupid.
- If you fail, it will devastate you. I can't handle that.

If he is harboring any of these fears, his negative reaction is understandable. He will need your love and reassurance more than ever.

Rabid Raccoon Remarks

And finally, here are some downright rude comments that may have spewed out of his mouth because of unchecked emotion.

- That's an absolutely idiotic idea.

- People will think you're crazy. I think you're crazy!

- You're not smart enough.

- What makes you think you could achieve something like that?

- You don't have what it takes.

- We'll go bankrupt in a month.

- Are you kidding me? Tell me you aren't really that stupid.

- Who do you think you are?

- Oh, geesh. What a loser.

- You've never succeeded at anything before- what makes you think this would be any different?

- You are such a sucker!

- There's no way you could ever accomplish that.

If any of these comments were shouted or accompanied by spastic laughter, the barbs can hurt even worse if you let them. But remember, while you aren't in control of your dream-killer's reaction, you ARE in control of how they affect you.

It's YOUR dream seed. It's YOUR gift. YOU can do whatever you have the fortitude to do. Period.

I wish I had known that a decade ago.

When I presented my MLM business to my husband, he laughed so hard, he started foaming at the mouth. Okay, maybe not exactly, but I felt that would be the next phase as he morphed into this vicious fiend, yelling some of the comments listed above.

He also made fun of the company, spitting out uninformed falsehoods and accusations. Hurt and anger filled me. I allowed myself to be swallowed up in emotion. Of course, I cried, which rendered me voiceless. The more I sputtered, the worse he got. I finally ran out of the room with dramatic flair.

Hopefully, that didn't happen to you. You were more prepared.

It wasn't until years later that I realized Hubby erupted with Rabid Raccoon Remarks as an automatic defense mechanism. He didn't really believe I was stupid or a loser. At least, I don't think so. But he felt he had to mask some unexpressed fears. He was too macho to admit vulnerability, not realizing that if he disclosed his true concerns, I would have understood. It actually would have endeared him to me.

Thankfully, I've learned a lot since then.

When presenting my second real estate investment (the first I had accomplished completely without his knowledge), I was calm, almost matter-of-fact about it. No long explanation, no pleading for understanding, and definitely no tears.

I'll admit, I had butterflies in my stomach and was braced for a deluge of negativity. Perhaps because I presented it in "C" mode, my hubby didn't argue or run me down. He didn't make fun of me. He just said, "Oh," and I walked away.

Not long after, I invited him (without expectancy) to see the four-unit dwelling I had just purchased. Surprisingly, he came. He recognized that I was going to fix up the place with or without him, so he chose to step into my world. I was able to drop the "C" and by the end of the tour, some of my "I" rubbed off on him. It was an awesome day.

Hubby even volunteered to do some remodeling work so I wouldn't have to hire a repairman. He has saved me (us) literally thousands of dollars. His support didn't come out of a desire for me to be in real estate investing. It's because we love each other.

And you? If your passion presentation brought you negative emotions, I encourage you to let them go. Concentrate on the good in your dream-killer and proceed to nurture your dream seed. As my grandmother used to say, "It will all come out in the wash."

What are your thoughts?

- Do you intend to present your dream to him again at some point?
- When?
- How?
- Or should you just be a unipreneur without efforts to include him?
- At least for now?

There are no right or wrong answers to these questions. It's totally up to you. You can throw your fishing line into the water again today. You can toss the whole pole in the trash. Or anything in between. Your call. But whatever you choose, please decide with a cool head and a calm heart.

ACTION STEPS

For Your Passion:

- Write down everything you remember about your passion presentation. What you both said, how you felt during and after, the expressions on his face, his body language, whatever else that impressed itself upon your memory. Don't edit it, just write freely.

- This may seem like a strange action to take for your passion, but I challenge you to take some time to rejuvenate. Do something you enjoy but don't often do. Go on a nature walk, visit a museum, have lunch with some friends that you haven't seen in a while, get a massage - whatever would help you completely step away from your dream-killer and your passion presentation for a few hours. Relax.

- Revisit your dream journal and/or your vision board. Fan the flames of your passion. Take time to envision yourself succeeding. What does it look like? How do you feel? Who is it helping? Breathe deeply and soak it all in. Success is yours!

- Write down at least 10 specific actions you could take to move forward with your dream that would take less than half an hour to complete. Start a practice of doing at least one of those a day, adding more to the list as new ideas come to you. This is a true success habit. All the little steps can eventually take you up the mountain.

For Your Relationships:

- Now that you've taken a mental break from your passion presentation, go back to read what you wrote in the first Action Step (For Your Passion) with fresh eyes. Consider carefully your dream-killer's negative responses. Determine if they came from inconsideration, misunderstanding, fear, or a combination of those.

- Without judgment, seek to understand what in history (his story) reinforces his negative response. If you can, ask leading questions to guide a civil discussion about his reaction to your passion presentation, do so if you desire. If not, feel free to completely withdraw from any further discussion about the topic until you feel moved to address it again. The timing is completely up to you.

PART III

PURSUE

Onward Expansion

Your dream has been given life. Your dream-killer has had the opportunity to give support (or not) and you are ready to ramp up the hot pursuit of your passion. You are now an official unipreneur! And while that means building your dream solo in the house, it does NOT mean doing it completely alone. In this section, I will share the importance of pursuing your dream with a network of supporters (including a mentor), developing personal character, and advancing on your journey toward success.

CHAPTER 7

BUILD YOUR NETWORK

"The key is to keep company only
with people who uplift you,
whose presence calls forth your best."

—Epictetus

According to the late Jim Rohn, you are the average of the five people you associate with the most. That doesn't mean you have to completely cut yourself off from every negative person in your life, but it does mean you need to find a network of like-minded individuals who will uplift and encourage you.

This is especially important since you have chosen to be a unipreneur AND stay with your dream-killer.

In spite of your loved one's adverse reaction, you've committed to nurture your dream, pursue your passion. You'll do it on your own. But that doesn't mean you have to BE alone. A strong support network will help you stay on your upward course.

Choose Your Friends Wisely

When you were a kid, did your mom or dad ever get upset with some of the friends you brought home? What about someone you dated? If not, you're fortunate, but I'll bet you at least had a sibling or friend in that situation.

I know my mother got some gray hairs when I was about 13. Middle school had introduced me to a whole new world of young people that weren't raised with the same Christian values my parents taught. I was exposed to alcohol, drugs, promiscuity - things that hadn't even been on my radar until that point.

Remember, this was in prehistoric times before the Internet. I didn't participate in those activities, but I was fascinated by my new friends who did.

However, I did find that my previously clean language became increasingly smudged from hanging out with my new, foul-mouthed cohorts. I didn't intend for that to happen; it came naturally as I rubbed shoulders with them.

School wasn't the problem. Rules were strict and all but the worst kids stuck to them. You could even get sent to the principal's office for just swearing. Imagine that! I know boys with more serious offenses got "licks" with a heavy, wooden paddle. I never heard of that happening to a girl, but I don't know if it was because of gender or a lack of serious offense. Gender was respected and unchangeable back then. Different world from today, I know.

The issues in my personal life happened beyond school hours.

I found it uncomfortable to have any of my new friends at my house for any length of time because I was afraid they'd swear (or something worse) in front of Mom or Dad. My parents had never said to me, "Laura, don't swear." They didn't have to. I knew in my gut what was appropriate in my home and what was not.

Again, it was the power of association. When I was with my family, I kept their standards. The more I was with my friends, the more I adopted theirs. So, I increasingly spent afternoons and weekends at my friends' houses where their parents didn't seem to care what we did.

Then I met my first "real" boyfriend, an older boy experienced with girls and rough life. I'll call him Ricky, although that isn't his real name. I seriously doubt he'll ever read this book, but just in case he changed the course of his life in later years, I wouldn't want to cause embarrassment.

We met through one of my new friends. When we weren't together at her house or the skating rink, Ricky and I were on the phone. Constantly. I was afraid for my parents to see him so I purposely didn't invite him to my house.

We didn't have any of the same classes at school. I was a nearly straight-A student (thank you, math, you messed up my 4.0), and Ricky was … well, he passed. He was one of the boys I mentioned who got licks in the principal's office. I remember the shocked looks when he started walking me to class. Then holding my hand. Then cuddling me under his arm.

One day while on the phone, Ricky told me he had a surprise. He had arranged for one of his car-owning buddies to drop him off at my house for a couple of hours that afternoon. He wanted to see me on my own turf.

I was thrilled and panicked at the same time. Not sure how my mom would react, I quickly invited our mutual friend to come to my house, too, so it wouldn't be obvious that Ricky was my boyfriend. He made it before our friend did. I remember being puzzled by his comment when I met him on the front porch.

"Wow. This is a mansion."

It wasn't a mansion. It was a modest three-bedroom, two-bath house with four kids inside. Later when I saw where Ricky lived, a tiny trailer with his mom and two brothers, I understood his remark.

Our mutual friend came shortly after, but it didn't fool my mother. She spied Ricky kiss me on the trampoline in the back yard. Oops.

That's when Mom started getting those gray hairs I was talking about. She didn't take long to figure out that I had been sneaking around. It became apparent why I had ditched Wednesday night church and sometimes even missed out on a Sunday service.

She wasn't mean or mad or anything negative. A truly great mother, she showed me love but shared her concern. I didn't accept her admonitions immediately, but tucked them in the back of my brain.

In spite of Ricky's well-earned bad reputation, he was always a gentleman in my presence. He showed me great respect and never pressured me to do anything illegal, immoral, or destructive even though that was often his personal pattern.

As a matter of fact, one time in the skating rink parking lot, a young man offered me a cigarette. Ricky slapped it out of his hand, shoved him in the chest, and spouted something like, "You ever offer one of those things to her again, and I'll punch your lights out!"

Ricky wouldn't have let me drink alcohol or do drugs, either. I was actually grateful for that because it gave me an excuse not to get involved in things I really didn't want to do. I could tiptoe on the edge of danger but he would keep me safe.

He controlled himself to kisses only, although he let me know that wasn't easy for him. He told me I was "pure" and he wanted me to stay that way. He was my protector.

One night at the skating rink, there was a new element of bad. A couple of guys showed up with hard drugs. Something clicked in my head, or perhaps stirred within my heart. I saw that I was walking a very fine line and was dangerously close to falling (or getting pushed) off to the darker side.

I stepped back to observe my "friends." While I liked them, even loved them, as people, I didn't like what they were doing. I was uncomfortable with the direction they were headed. I didn't want to go along with them anymore.

And what about Ricky? I really loved the guy as much as a 13-year-old heart is capable. He treated me like I was a delicate treasure. But I knew we couldn't stay together. What was a girl to do?

I turned to God. Dusting off the Bible that I hadn't bothered to read for a while, the book literally fell open in my hands to Matthew 6:22. It said: *"The light of the body is the eye: if therefore thine eye be single, thy whole body shall be full of light."*

A warm light flowed over me. I stopped for several minutes, closing my eyes to soak it in. It was sweet, fulfilling, joyful.

I continued to the next verse: *"But if thine eye be evil, thy whole body shall be full of darkness. If therefore the light that is in thee be darkness, how great is that darkness!"*

Cold blackness oozed through me like ice in my veins. It was as dark as the light had been bright. I knew in my heart what I wanted to do. I committed my life to Jesus Christ that very moment. It changed me.

I shared my newfound faith with my friends, but it wasn't well received. No surprise. I slipped out of their world and into one with a new set of Christian youth that became forever friends.

And Ricky? He responded by getting drunk and waking up in bed with a girl from one of my classes, not remembering how he got there. At least that's what he told me in confessional form. It hurt both of us, but it made the split easier.

The friends at church were positive and upwardly mobile in every way. So was I. My new network of support upheld me in my new, light-filled course. There was no desire to go back to Ricky or his crowd. As Jim Rohn said, I became like my five best friends.

How about you? Do have a positive tribe to encourage you to be your best self? Is there a continual source of encouragement for your passion?

Truth is, adults are influenced by peer pressure just as we were in our younger years. It may not be as intense, but it's always present. Associations can lift you up or tear you down. Which will you choose?

Look in the Mirror

You reflect who you hang out with. If you spend every weekend drinking with your buddies, watching sports, playing video games, or gossiping with friends on social media, guess what? That's who you are.

If you invest your down-time with people that have deep, enlightening conversations (in person or online), and continually want to improve themselves, guess what? That's who you are.

Not saying you can't watch sports or have fun with friends, we ALL need some rest and relaxation, but if that's where all your discretionary time goes, don't expect to live an expansive life.

When my hubby lost his faith, I let myself feel completely alone and isolated for several years. It was a dark, rough road. Because I'm people-oriented, I kept my sanity by keeping and developing relationships with people from church, Girl Scouts, 4-H, and community volunteer groups. Folks that basically had my same desire to serve others.

But I didn't share my deep aspirations. I stuck my dream seeds in a stony place because I didn't see a way for them to grow. I survived but I didn't thrive.

In my mid-40's, I remember thinking, "I'm going to be 50 soon. Is this it? Is this as good as my life will ever be?"

It wasn't that I had a horrible life. I didn't. Especially compared to what I read about in headlines or saw on TV. But my life was so different than I had expected that I had a hard time visualizing a grand future. I was stuck in that bitter field of regret. I had settled for mediocrity.

Being introduced to my MLM company was a Godsend. I'm forever grateful to our daughter who shared it with me. The company itself is not my dream, but it provided three crucial elements that encouraged me on the journey to live my passion.

First, it provided a personal development system which not only encouraged me to rejuvenate my dream seeds, but gave me the know-how and tools to grow them. Second, it provided a vehicle to become financially free. And third, it provided a tribe of upwardly mobile associates and successful mentors to show me the way.

No Need to Be a Lone Ranger

Being a unipreneur in your home doesn't mean you have to do everything by yourself! Even the Lone Ranger had Tonto.

I can't adequately express what a difference it makes to be around expansive people who have passions in their lives.

My eyes open each morning with gratitude and expectation. Life is exciting!

When I first shared my newfound opportunity with my husband and he ridiculed me mercilessly, my MLM tribe had my back. They comforted me, encouraged me, and celebrated every little step. As a matter of fact, they walked along side me. Even if I had decided to quit the business, they would have supported my choice.

In turn, I have done the same for them. We are like family. Every one of us have gone through major challenges and we help each other in whatever way we can. We each have had successes, which we also celebrate together. It's awesome to be part of such an uplifting group.

And as our businesses continue to grow, so do our connections. Our association just gets bigger and stronger.

I already asked you this, but because it's so important, I'm going to ask again. Do you already have a support group?

I'm not referring to friends that just listen to you share problems and then agree how bad things are. Or people who try to out-do everything you say.

I'm talking about friends that truly listen in order to understand. They want you to have, do, and be your best. If they see a problem (or potential problem), they aren't afraid to tell you, but they don't just gripe about it, they help find answers and solutions. And you do the same for them.

If you aren't part of such a group, start right now to find or build one.

Where? How? It depends on your passion.

A horse jockey hangs around stables, race tracks, and other jockeys. While he probably has other interests which don't involve equine, I seriously doubt he spends all his spare time at a golf course.

Go where people who share your passion meet. Congregate with them. If you can't find a physical place, go online. Use social media to find other like-minded individuals.

If nothing particularly suits you, start a group yourself. YOU be the magnet. I have no doubt that if you open your heart and mind, you will attract Godsend individuals into your life.

My guess is, you may already know at least one positive friend or family member that you can trust with your passion. Someone who can keep confidences. And perhaps he, too, has a dream seed itching to sprout. That's even better.

If it feels right, start there. Just share a little at first to see how he reacts. Share as much and as quickly as you want. You might be surprised how thrilled your cohort will be if the fit is right. Then grow your group.

AN IMPORTANT WORD OF CAUTION: If your main dream-killer is also your spouse/life-partner, please heed this warning. As you cultivate new relationships and strengthen existing ones, be careful not to develop inappropriate attractions to any individuals. Remember the premise is to be a unipreneur AND be faithful to your dream-killer.

Share your dreams but not the details of struggles with your dream-killer. Focus on the good. Countless illicit affairs have started because of allowing improper gravitation toward a sympathetic somebody. However small it starts, consider this: If your significant other felt that same emotion toward someone other than you, how would you feel? Uncomfortable? Hurt? Jealous? If so, nip it in the bud! Always try to live by the Golden Rule.

Don't put yourself in a position where the flames of scandalous desire are flamed. Stay with a group. If you need to meet with an individual with whom there is personal attraction, stay in a public, well-lit location. That's good advice, even if there isn't apparent attraction. You may be unaware that the individual has attractions to YOU. Simple caution may save you from deep regret.

Stop the Elevator

I wish I could give credit to the unknown person who said "Life is like an elevator. On your way up, you have to stop to let some people off."

By now, you should already have a good idea which of your friends you need to let off. Perhaps some have already left. Or maybe you chose to exit the elevator yourself in order to find another one in an entirely different building. One with more floors. How about a skyscraper?

If relatives are invading your space, you may have to pick and choose which family gatherings to attend. When there is an all-day barbecue, arrive late and leave early. A birthday party? Take a present, sing Happy Birthday, but when the negative conversation starts up, kindly excuse yourself and head for the hills. Give as much face time as you deem necessary to keep off their black list, but not enough to suck out your soul.

That can be especially tricky if it's your dream-killer's clan. Or his work associates. Sometimes you have to ride the lift together for a little while, but remember it's temporary.

Personally, there's a handy little game I play in those situations. When negative statements or ideas get flung around, I interject something positive. I don't make a big deal of it, just state it simply. Sometimes my words are serious and provoke thought. Other times I use humor to lighten the conversation.

My comments often start with either "At least ..." or "Better than ...". For example:

- Uncle Joe and Cousin Vicky are topping each other's stories about their horrible jobs. I say, "At least you're both employed. You can afford a roof over your head and food on the table."

- My dream-killer and his colleagues are griping about the price of gas and the greedy oil companies. I say, "Better than having to roller skate everywhere. Have you ever skated pulling a little red wagon full of groceries? Not fun."

If nothing else, my comments usually keep the negativity from escalating further. But sometimes it actually derails it. That gives me time to escape the train before it gets on the downward track again.

Identify Your Mentors

Once you cull out your negative associations and get in tight with your new, positive tribe, keep your eyes open for someone who's already successful at what you want to do. Connect with him. When you find a match who's willing, be his student, his apprentice, his understudy, even his flunky if that's what it takes. Like a sponge, soak in all you can learn and put it into practice.

If your dream is to blaze a trail for others, you can still get to that point more efficiently if you find someone willing to teach you success principles. Use their expertise as a springboard to live your own passion.

When I connected with my MLM, I found it invaluable that my upline chose to guide me in building my personal business. Yes, I realize that by helping me, their businesses also grew, but it was more than that. They sincerely wanted me to flourish. They showed me that if I stuck to the proven system of the MLM, I could succeed without wasting time with trial and error methods that had already been tested. They showed me, step by step, how they achieved their success.

Much later, when I had some seed money to pursue another income source (real estate investing), I again found a network of positive people who knew the business and were willing (and eager) to teach me. I took a series of courses on locating properties, wholesaling, rehabbing, flipping, hard money lending, aspects of being a land lord, and property management. But I couldn't seem to make myself actually buy any property. Truth is, I was scared.

I realized I needed a mentor. Ironically, I met him at an MLM conference where he was the main speaker. Like many successful people, he had more than one business, but at least some of his millions had come from real estate.

His name? Omar Periu. I invested in six months of one-on-one mentorship with him. Through his tutelage, I gained the know-how and self-confidence to make my first real estate purchase. That was just the beginning.

During my time with Omar, something even greater happened than becoming a real estate investor. He challenged me to look deep within myself to discover my true passion. Was it real estate? No. That brought me a limited amount of satisfaction, but it didn't give me joy. I didn't wake up each morning yelling, "Whoo-hoo! What piece of property am I going to find today?"

I had met others who DID have that as their passion. But it wasn't mine. Deep inside, I knew that I wanted to write. I even made a declaration in front of Omar and other students that someday I was going to write a book.

Someday. Hmm ... that didn't exactly light the fire under me. Something held me back from pursuing it. I wasn't sure what.

In the final months of Omar's mentorship, I was drawn to an advertisement for an online coaching program by Life Coach, Mary Manin Morrissey, as part of Life Mastery Institute. It was early December. I told my husband not to buy me a Christmas gift, that I was going to buy my own.

I immediately purchased the 12-week Dreambuilder course and didn't wait for the holidays to start the modules. It changed the trajectory of my life. I became a student of Mary's and had the pleasure of having one of her best coaches, Kirsten Welles, as my mentor for a year.

It was during my time with Life Mastery Institute that I took my dream seed of becoming a published author off the back shelf and set it in the light. I discovered a negative paradigm that had stopped me. I mistakenly believed that my desire to write was selfish.

After all, how could something that brought me such delight be beneficial to anyone else? Right?

Wrong! I finally realized that my deep, persistent desire to write was a gift from God, a gift to be developed and shared.

Not just the occasional magazine article or short story I had published sporadically over the years. Not just writing copy for others. Books, both fiction and non-fiction, screenplays, teleplays, courses to help people improve their lives ... YES! I'm not just a writer, I'm a creator. I am a word weaver.

Again, toward the end of my time with Life Mastery Institute, Providence led me to yet another mentor: writing coach, Kary Oberbrunner. It's through Kary's guidance that this book is a reality. And it's only the first. My only regret is that it's taken me this long to live my passion.

What about your passion? Is it going to be another 10 years before you pursue it? Or are you ready to live it NOW?

I challenge you to find your tribe, your network of dream-builders with whom you share support.

To speed up your journey and hopefully make it less painful, find someone who has already traveled the path and achieved what you want to do, a qualified mentor that shares your values. Choose only one mentor at a time, two at the most. Stick with them for at least six months to a year. Laser focus on what is taught and then boldly apply it in your life. Regardless of your situation at home, your positive associates can help propel you toward your dream.

You're on your way!

ACTION STEPS

For Your Passion:

- Carefully observe your circle of friends and weed out the negative ones who drain you.

- Find and connect with people who share your passion. This can be in person, online, or both.

- Evaluate your relationships with family members. Limit time with those who drag you down. When it's necessary to be in their presence, find positive things to counteract their negative conversations.

- Locate a mentor who can help guide you to the next level of growth. Make sure you share the same values and that you "click" with one another.

For Your Relationships:

- Recommit yourself to complete fidelity to your significant other. Don't get in a situation that might lead to unfaithfulness.

- Spend time with your dream-killer doing something neither one of you has done before. Decide together what you will do or where you will go. The discussion can bring you closer and so can the activity itself. Afterward, have another discussion to evaluate the experience. What did you love about it? What would you change?

CHAPTER 8

BUILD YOUR CHARACTER

"Man's mind, once stretched by a new idea,
never regains its original dimensions."

—Oliver Wendell Holmes

I'm fortunate that my MLM has a dynamic personal
development system as part of its offerings. After years
of trudging through the same old muck, it set me on an
upward trajectory that I never intend to stop.

You, too, can exponentially increase your learning by taking
advantage of others' experiences. Compound interest, so to
speak. As you constantly stimulate your mind with expansive ideas, you become a better YOU. Thus, all the good in
your life is magnified.

That's what all this is about, isn't it? Becoming the best unipreneur possible? Nurturing that God-given dream seed and
developing it into a life of passion?

Dang, life is awesome when you're headed in the right direction!

The Big Picture

Before I go into specifics of building your character, I want to glimpse a larger view. It's a basic premise of life as expressed by Mary Morrissey in her Dreambuilder program.

Mary teaches that there are four areas in which each of us continually live:

- Health & Wellness
- Relationships
- Vocation
- Time & Money Freedom

In the *Life Mastery* program, we focused on improving and expanding on one of those areas, such as health & wellness, for a month. We then concentrated on relationships for a month. Then vocation and, finally, time & money freedom. The process would then repeat. However, while focusing on one area, we never neglected ANY of the other areas. Thus, our lives continually improved in a balanced way.

It was not just a year-long program for me. It was a new pattern for the rest of my life.

Have you ever seen a "successful" person who was healthy and rich but had terrible relationships? Or someone so focused on their career for an extended period of time that their health fell apart? They were continually out of balance.

Each of these areas need nurturing, even when focused on one or two.

We are not static beings. That is, we are in a spiral of life going either upward or downward. If you aren't moving up or down, then you're just going around in a circle, but you're still moving.

As Mary says, "Some people live 90 years. Some people live the same year 90 times." I'm guilty of living the same year for about a decade or so, around and around and around like a mule turning a millstone. I'm SO grateful that's history.

If that's been your life, it's okay. Don't kick yourself. Just start moving upward today.

Stay on Course

I've loved to canoe since I was 10 years old. I discovered it at a Girl Scout camp on the shores of Lake Texoma, which is one of the largest reservoirs in the United States. It has over 93,000 acres of surface area and boasts an elongated, jagged shoreline of approximately 550 miles.

Having a natural affinity with American Indians (yes, I know that isn't a politically correct term, but I'm part Cherokee and it's what I prefer. To me, anybody born in the U.S. is a native American), I loved to pretend I was in a dugout, heading for a Pow-Wow on one of the islands that dotted the lake.

Did you notice my sidetracked comment in the middle of that last sentence? It's what Mary calls "drift." It's typical as human beings to frequently veer off course. What's empowering is to notice it as soon as it happens and correct the route immediately before we end up where we don't want to go.

My first realization of drift in a physical sense was as a teenager canoeing on Lake Texoma. Two adventuresome and dedicated Girl Scout leaders took four of us Cadettes and three canoes "island hopping" for a full week. We packed light because all our gear and food had to fit in between each pair of paddlers. Back in those ancient days, the islands and the shores were still "wild" territory, with the exception of a few campgrounds and lakeside homes.

It was before cell phones or GPS capabilities; we were completely on our own. A compass and the position of the sun were our guides. North was Oklahoma, south was Texas. We planned to stop at the six main islands from west to east, and back again. That was enough to know.

Leaving the Texas embankment early in the morning, we headed for West Island to have lunch and play in the water. When rested, we paddled east to Wooded Island to set up camp, cook dinner, and sleep under the stars. The second day, we navigated to Hog Island for lunch and Treasure Island for the night. Third day was Little Island and North Island. Each time we left an island, we followed the compass until the next island was in sight.

Our idea was to sleep on a different one of the main islands each night. That meant on the morning of the fourth day, we relaxed on North Island until after lunch. After being true to our motto "leave things better than you found them," and thus disposing of all evidence of our little campsite, we were back in our canoes.

When Little Island was in view, we put the compass away, as had become our habit. After all, we were old pros by then. For a short period of time, we quit paddling. Singing camp songs, goofing around, general silliness, I don't remember the specifics.

However, I DO remember someone saying, "Hey! Where's the island?"

We all stopped messing around. The island had vanished. One of the girls pointed and said, "That way!"

After an hour or two of paddling "that way," all we could see was the Oklahoma shoreline. Ugh.

Later, I realized our leaders always knew our exact location but they didn't let on. A golden opportunity for hands-on learning had presented itself. At the time, I thought they were lost, too.

"What do you want to do?" asked one of the leaders. "Keep looking for an island? Or camp in Oklahoma?

After a short discussion, we headed back into the lake. Eventually, we spotted an island and landed. It obviously was not Little Island. We dubbed it Much Littler Island and unloaded our gear. Hungry and sore-armed, we wanted to set up camp before dark.

Around the crackling campfire that night, we discussed what had happened. We had taken our eyes off the goal and strayed just a little in the wrong direction. Because of a slight drift in our route, we ended up at an entirely different destination. Instead of sleeping where we intended, we were on an island so tiny, you could stand up and see water in every direction. It didn't even have an official name.

That trip occurred over 40 years ago. Given the current condition of our society, I can't imagine letting any of our daughters go canoeing with a group of girls for a week, not knowing exactly where they were and without instant communication. But four decades ago, it was an awesome experience. It pushed us both physically and mentally, stretching us into more empowered individuals.

The moral of the story? Be aware of drift and continually adjust your course.

Perpetual Growth

To live your passion, especially with a dream-killer in your house, you will need to be vigilant in enlarging yourself. No, I don't mean to gain 100 pounds. I mean to expand your mind, your spirit, your experience.

How?

Besides hanging out with big achievers, the most obvious method is to read. This book, for instance.

If you've been reading with an open mind and engaging in the Action Steps, you are MORE than you were when you started. You are learning from my experiences so you can get a head-start in living your passion regardless of who tries to dampen your enthusiasm.

Reading can catapult you on the learning curve of life.

I love the words of English author, Joseph Addison, penned almost 300 years ago, but just as valid today: "Reading is to the mind what exercise is to the body."

You will always find a book in my purse, my car, my computer bag, my desk, anywhere that I may find a spare moment between tasks. You will also find different digital books on all my electronic devices.

To me, every minute is valuable. There are no do-overs. Once I've traded a minute of my life for something, there is no getting it back. So even a paragraph of educational or uplifting words is golden.

My MLM company has a voluntary program in which a recommended book and a set of audios are offered each month. I've been involved in that for almost a decade. I've improved myself one book, one audio at a time and the results are fulfilling.

It has given me the inner strength to nurture my dream seed regardless of circumstances. It's allowed me to love my main in-house dream-killer without trying to change him.

Although my body ages each year, my mind continues to expand and, with it, the joy of the journey. I never want to get to a point where I say, "Okay, I've arrived. I've learned all I need to know, so I'm going to stop growing. I'm good enough so I'll quit trying to improve."

If you ever hear me say that, just throw me in a coffin.

Please don't think I'm saying my every waking hour is grand and expansive. They aren't. I make stupid mistakes every single day. And yes, I meant the word mistakes to be plural.

Rude drivers still make my blood pressure spike. Inconsiderate words still slip from my lips, causing anger or hurt. Sometimes, I still let myself get exasperated when Hubby talks over me when I'm speaking. I still have times when I escape into a movie or computer game instead of facing a challenge. I still, I still, I still ...

The difference is, I now recognize those behaviors more readily and have the desire to change them. I don't beat myself up over mistakes but let them go, then try to correct my thoughts and actions. Baby steps upward. Hopefully, my character will continually improve bit by bit.

So, what do I mean by the word "character"?

The sixth definition for character in the Merriam-Webster Dictionary is: moral excellence and firmness; example: *a man of sound character.* In Dictionary.com, the third definition is: moral or ethical quality: example: *a man of fine, honorable character,* and the fourth definition is: qualities of honesty, courage, or the like; integrity; example; *It takes character to face up to a bully.*

That's what I mean. Here are some characteristics I believe a person should try to develop to move upward on the spiral of life. These positive traits are desirable in the pursuit of your passion. The list is by no means exhaustive and some of the meanings may overlap or have only subtle differences. Wanting to give each equal value, I simply put them in alphabetical order.

Accountable	Energetic	Optimistic
Approachable	Enthusiastic	Patient
Authentic	Ethical	Polite
Balanced	Faithful	Pleasant
Compassionate	Generous	Receptive
Considerate	Genuine	Respectful
Consistent	Harmonious	Responsible
Conscientious	Honest	Sincere
Creative	Incorruptible	Steadfast
Dependable	Innovative	Tactful
Determined	Joyful	Tenacious
Encouraging	Observant	Trustworthy

I know that's a lot but please don't be overwhelmed. I'm sure you already exhibit some, if not many, of those characteristics. Choose one or a related two or three to concentrate on at first. Remember, one step at a time.

The expectation should not be perfection. It should be continual improvement.

There are a few other characteristics that have caveats. They warrant brief discussion. Again, I'll list them alphabetically.

Adventuresome but not reckless - To grow, we should be willing to try new things, consider unorthodox options, explore fresh approaches. But that doesn't mean to bungee jump without measuring the cord!

Don't put yourself in harm's way out of curiosity or just to prove a point. Don't put others in peril, either. And I'm not just talking about physical danger. It could be financial, spiritual, relational, whatever.

Will you take risks while living your passion? Absolutely. There is risk every time you move out of the safety of the familiar. But you can reduce the chance of harmful consequences by being as aware as possible. You don't want to get stuck forever analyzing a situation but at least peruse the possibilities, scan the scene, take quick inventory before acting.

Jumping out of an airplane with a parachute is an acceptable risk to some. Checking to make sure the parachute is packed correctly and having a backup reduce the risk considerably. Leaping off the plane before securing the harness? That's reckless!

<u>Assertive but not aggressive</u> - Should you offer your opinions, services, or actions when appropriate? Yes. But do it in a positive, non-threatening way. Winning someone over by confidently sharing your ideas is much more powerful than getting things done through fear tactics. Force does not win friends and loyal supporters. But it does make phony friends and seething enemies.

Remember that aggression comes from a scarcity mindset. It's the notion that there isn't enough to go around so you must grab it before someone else does.

For example, over two decades ago, we opened our home to two children ages 4 and 7, for a couple of weeks in the summer while their parents went out of state on a job search. Their six other siblings had been farmed out to other families. Tremendous financial turmoil had plagued them for several years as evidenced by the actions of the 7-year-old, whom I will fictitiously call Julie.

We had five children of our own at the time and it was our custom to sit around the dining room table together at each meal, not just dinner. Before eating, we'd bow our heads and close our eyes as someone offered a prayer of thanks and asked for a divine blessing on the food.

Although our little guests' first meal with us was lunch, I made pancakes and small link sausages. It was quick, easy, relatively cheap, and I didn't know a kid that didn't like pancakes. My husband was at work.

One of our older boys said the prayer and when we opened our eyes, we had an awkward moment of shock and disbelief. While our eyes had been closed, Julie had silently stacked all of the sausages and half the pancakes on her and her little brother's plates. She was in the process of slathering it with margarine and had the syrup bottle between her knees.

One of our younger sons finally grumbled, "No fair! We want some sausages, too!"

Julie protectively threw her arms over her plate. She might have even hissed.

"It's okay," I said, getting up to return to the griddle. "I'll make more pancakes."

By the end of lunch, Julie and her brother had snarfed all the sausages but their stomachs were so full, they couldn't stuff in all the pancakes they had piled up. Already drenched in syrup, I had to throw them away.

Afterward, I had to have a little talk with Julie. It went something like this:

"Sweetie, we don't like to waste food in our house, so we have a rule that you only put on your plate what you know you can eat. Just take a little so there's enough for everyone to have some."

No response. Just a blank stare.

"Like the sausages. Because all of them were on your plate – and your brother's - none of the rest of the kids got any."

She looked at me like I was speaking Chinese.

"Next time we eat, wait until the food is passed to you and just put a little on your plate. Then you can have seconds."

Finally, she spoke. "What are seconds?"

"A second helping. It means after you eat what you put on your plate the first time, you can get more if you're still hungry."

Her eyes got big. "We don't have seconds at our house."

I realized she was aggressive because in her world, if she didn't snatch food before her older siblings, she may not get enough to appease her growling belly. She was also providing for her younger brother who she felt was too little to fend for himself. It was a bi-product of scarcity.

<u>Diplomatic but not dishonest</u> - If your friend asks you, "Does this make me look fat?", there is no need to say, "YES!" (truth) or "No." (lie). There are truthful alternatives such as, "I prefer the black skirt (or the loose blouse or whatever your think looks better)." I know that's a trivial

example, but you get the drift. Dishonesty, even in the guise of consideration, leads to distrust.

This will be especially important as you pursue your passion without your dream-killer actively on your support team while at the same time staying in a close relationship with him. Diplomacy will help keep the peace. Dishonesty will destroy it.

Friendly but not intrusive - Being cordial is one thing, acting friendly to the point of invading personal space is another. As an I/S personality type, I enjoy people, but I still get uncomfortable when someone talks so close to my face that I can detect what they ate for breakfast. You probably do, too.

As your network expands and new friendships develop, respect boundaries. Don't sit smack next to a new acquaintance, gush out your life story, and expect him to reciprocate. Be congenial, smile, open yourself to conversation, but be aware of and honor other people's privacy zones.

Humble but not timid - I love the following quote by the late Jim Rohn: "Some people mistake timidity for humility. But humility is a virtue; timidity is a disease."

This includes self-effacing thoughts and speech. In years past, I was guilty of this. Somehow, I thought if I expressed something positive about myself, I would be conceited, so I went the other direction. I frequently articulated my short-comings. Compliments were rebuffed with, "Thanks, but I'm not _____." That paradigm did absolutely nothing to improve myself or anyone else.

Resist the urge to debunk compliments. Accept them with grace and gratitude. True, you aren't worth more than anyone else but neither are you any less valuable.

<u>Humorous but not silly</u> - It's great to have a sense of humor. I'd go so far as to say it's critical to maintain a positive view. However, there are proper times and places to have fun. Continual slapstick silly can be a complete turn-off.

Want an extreme example?

A friend of mine is a stand-up comedian. I knew her long before she hit the stage and she was always fun to be around. Besides a keen sense of humor, she offered great insight on a variety of topics including her husband and kids, appreciating nature, her faith in God.

Now I find it hard to carry on a conversation with her. Everything is a potential joke, including personal communications. Nothing is sacred. It cost her a marriage. Her children (adults now) are afraid to confide in her for fear it might be adapted into a comic routine. Grandkids? Kept a safe distance away.

While I can't judge what's in her heart, she appears to be addicted to silliness. She's currently so driven by a need for manic laughter, both in the spotlight and off, that all other areas of her life seem to be neglected. I sincerely hope she seeks more balance soon before she topples over.

I don't suspect you are in the same situation. I'm not either. But we can still learn from my friend's experience. It's never okay to get a laugh at someone else's expense. Or your own, for that matter. Fun and laughter are cleansing and rejuvenating, but only when appropriate.

<u>Self-confident but not egotistical</u> - It's wonderful to know your great value, feel comfortable in your own skin, and take pride in your accomplishments. But it isn't okay to be arrogant about it. Remember, EACH PERSON has a unique gift to offer the world. While not everyone has remembered and developed their dream seeds yet, they are still integral in the tapestry of life. Each thread adds its own beauty.

Personally, I've found a key to resist becoming smug, even while on an amazing upward track. It's simple: sincerely serve others. Not just donating to non-profits or sharing expertise and opportunities (although those are important, too), but working in the trenches. Getting your hands dirty. Nothing is so equalizing as to labor side by side in a noble cause.

Other Resources for Personal Development

Besides reading great books, you can attend seminars and conferences that align with your passion. Listen intently. Participate fully. Take lots of notes. Go early and offer to help set up. Stay late and offer to clean up. You'll be surprised what extras you can learn in the after-hours.

Along with audio books, I also listen to speeches, talks, and podcasts. Downloaded on my electronic devices, they're perfect for when I'm doing household chores, walking, driving, or otherwise not able to read.

The Internet is filled with valuable information and visuals although you must use caution as to the sources. Remember to stay true to your course, keep your island in sight. It's easy to get diverted by side stories and distracting pictures. If you choose to surf the net as a means of relaxation, set a timer. Otherwise you may get caught in the drift for hours.

One of my favorite personal growth activities is attending free online webinars. I've learned basics on numerous topics relating to my businesses and personal development. I've also gained knowledge on other subjects that interest me such as different cultures, artistic pursuits, American History, the Constitution, and spiritual growth.

I've also started watching some webinars that I realized weren't what I expected. Yoink! I turned them off. No time or money wasted. You can do the same. It costs nothing to try them out. Just make sure you don't buy every program that is offered. Be prudent. Don't buy on impulse but if something deeply triggers your heart and energizes you to action, consider it.

A free webinar offered on Facebook is actually how I found my writing coach, Kary Oberbrunner. Through him, I clarified my vision and committed to write this book. I will close this chapter with a phrase that Kary encourages each of his students to embody, no matter where we are or what we're doing. It's a motto to help us get the most out of every minute we breath.

His words? "Show up filled up." Give it all you've got and you'll see amazing results!

ACTION STEPS

For Your Passion:

- Visit www.UnipreneurBook.com for a list of great books and authors. Choose one to start reading as soon as you finish this one.

- Find audios online, at your local library, or at www.UnipreneurBook.com that will expand your mind. Download onto a personal electronic device and listen to them during downtime such as waiting for an appointment or driving alone. Save your favorites to listen to multiple times.

- Carefully consider the list of positive characteristic traits. Honestly evaluate yourself to see which ones you are already exhibiting and which ones you need to work on. Choose one or a related two or three on which to concentrate. Seriously apply yourself to master them.

- Revisit the seven character traits with caveats. Think of a personal experience which could illustrate one of them.

For Your Relationships:

- Read the list of 36 character traits again, this time with your dream-killer in mind. Find at least three of them that he exhibits regularly. Next time you observe him demonstrating that quality, compliment him on it. Remember, only concentrate on his strengths. Don't pick those on which he needs to improve.

- Take a free online webinar or read a book on a topic important to your dream-killer that you know little about. Surprise him by starting a knowledgeable conversation on the subject.

CHAPTER 9

ADVANCE YOUR JOURNEY

"I have been impressed with the urgency of doing. Knowing is not enough; we must apply. Being willing is not enough; we must do."

—Leonardo da Vinci

With the vast amount of information literally at our fingertips today (thank you, Internet), it's possible to learn about an infinite number of subjects. A person could spend his entire life studying and still only absorb a small fraction of what's available.

That's a two-edged sword.

Knowledge can help you live your passion. Or it can sidetrack you from your quest. What good will it do if you spend the next 50 years learning about your chosen path (and a zillion other things) yet you never take a step forward?

A hermit may live in contentment, surrounded by his books and Internet, filling his mind with an incessant flow of data.

But in the end, does it help him reach his potential if he doesn't in some way share what he knows? What good is a song left unsung?

In other words, in your decision to be a unipreneur, be careful not to let yourself get bogged down with subject matter. Don't get so caught up learning about success that you neglect to act on it.

As I mentioned in the last chapter, I love to watch free webinars. There is SO much great content that sometimes it's difficult for me not to buy all the curricula offered at the end of each session. I admit there was a time that I bought several programs which, at first, I tried to do all at once. I bounced from one thing to another, one teacher to another.

The topics were related to my passion, different elements of the whole, but because my attention was so scattered, I wasn't able to act on what I learned. I increased my knowledge but became proficient at nothing.

It wasn't the most efficient use of my time or energy. Instead of feeling invigorated, I felt stressed and drained. I was drowning in content.

Another birthday rolled around, and I evaluated my life. I had more knowledge but had not become wiser. I hadn't put what I learned into practice.

Duh. No wonder I felt stressed. My thoughts were expansive but my actions didn't match. The incongruence crippled me. Instead of moving me forward, it held me back.

Once I finally recognized my self-inflicted diversion, all but one of the programs I had purchased were shelved. Not because they weren't great information or I lost interest, but because I realized that they were a distraction from my immediate course. I could only concentrate on one at a time if I planned to apply what I learned to my life.

Learn, then do. Go to the next program, next mentor, next step. Learn, then do. It's a pattern that works.

By the way, I still love free webinars. Instead of an occasional chill session in front of the TV, I much prefer to spend down-time gleaning from successful people with varying expertise.

For example, I watched one by T. Harv Eker only a few days ago that I absolutely loved. I almost signed up, even got my purse out to get my credit card. But I stopped myself, realizing it would interfere with my focus of getting this book done. If I would still love to have T. Harv Eker as a mentor after "Unipreneur" is in publication, then I will do it. But not until then and not unless it feels right.

And YOU must do what feels right for YOU.

Trust Yourself, Trust God

Did you or your kids ever watch the "He-Man and the Masters of the Universe" cartoon series? I can still envision muscle-bound He-Man holding his magic sword high in the air, his voice booming, "I HAVE THE POOOWERRR!!!

Truth is, we all have the power.

Hopefully, you're now more aware of your inner strength, your natural ability, your God-given right to choose your thoughts and actions. That awareness itself gives you more power than the average person. Most people, unfortunately, aren't yet conscious of their capabilities. But you are.

You no longer have to react willy-nilly to whatever comes your way. You know better. You don't have to let reactions control you, you can control them.

And with that new knowledge comes responsibility (the ability to respond). There is major disparity between reacting and responding. Reactions are driven by circumstances outside yourself. Responses are driven by conscious choice.

Now you understand the difference.

You are free to be whomever you want to be! You can choose to live your passion regardless of your conditions. That includes negativity from your dream-killers. You CAN succeed if you have the fortitude to advance. But you must trust your heart, your intuition, the whisperings of God in your mind.

That reminds me of a story.

When I was a kid, I loved to barrel race. I didn't have a fast horse, I never won anything in a rodeo, but I thought it was great fun.

I can still feel the movement of the galloping equine underneath me, hear the rhythm of the hooves hitting the dirt, see our approach to the first barrel. I remember tugging on the reins to get her as close as we could without knocking it over, rushing to circle the second barrel, and the third.

Then came the wild, straight, home stretch. I can still smell the lather foaming on my mare's neck as I bent over her, the breeze whipping my face as we raced to the finish line. That's the only time I gave her free rein to go as fast as she could. It was completely exhilarating!

Fast forward 30 years.

One of my nieces grew up on a horse, so to speak. She loved to barrel race, too. As a teenager, her dad bought her a beautiful black mare named Jet who was the retired barrel racing horse of a Texas champion. For years, Jet had lived and breathed barrel racing. It was in her blood.

One summer, I was visiting my sister in Texas, when my niece asked me if I'd like to ride her horse. Of course, I immediately said yes, even though I hadn't been riding in at least a decade, maybe more.

To my surprise, they had barrels set up just like a regulation race.

"Go for it, Aunt Laura!"

Excitement filled my veins as I positioned the horse to start. I leaned forward, clicking my teeth as a signal to take off.

"Jet" was a good name for her.

She bolted for the first barrel like a Lockheed YF-12. I had to grab the saddle horn with one hand to stay on (which is something barrel racers NEVER do), while pulling back on the reins with the other in a futile attempt to slow the pace. I felt totally out of control.

It quickly dawned on me that Jet knew exactly what she was doing. My guidance was unnecessary. In my attempt to take charge and make something happen, all I accomplished was to keep her from reaching the greatest potential. Choosing to trust her instead, I relaxed. I gave her full rein and let her GO!

It was amazing.

Once I quit trying to control her, the rhythm came, and it was much faster, a great deal smoother than I had ever experienced. We became one in purpose and the result was fantastic.

Jet now represents my inner self, my connection to God. We are all part of a divine, infinite source that wants us to succeed. Each of us are given treasures and tools to move us forward, but if those implements go unrecognized or misused, we won't achieve our utmost capability.

If we let our past experience rule how we act in the present without even considering a greater possibility, we will never reach our pinnacle. We may be content but we'll never be joyful. We may be good but we'll never be great.

I want to be joyful. I want to be great. And I think you do, too.

So, let go of trying to control all the conditions and put your trust in God. He will help you accomplish your goals with more grace, ease, and speed than you ever can on your own. And the ride will be awesome!

Failure Is Not a Nasty Word

Now that you're a unipreneur, you'll have to face the following fact: Failures will pop up here and there on your road to success. That isn't a maybe, it's inevitable. It isn't if, it's when. The failures themselves are not the issue, it's how you choose to deal with them. React? Or respond.

Yes, it's that choice-thing again.

First, let's identify some destructive or fruitless thoughts about failure:

- I failed, therefore I am a failure. I'm branded forever.
- I feel such pain (anger, embarrassment, whatever negative emotion) that I will never try again.
- Failure? What failure? There's no failure! (deny, deny, deny)
- It's his fault. It's her fault. It's everybody else's fault but mine. I'm totally blameless.
- Maybe it was just bad luck. I'm going to do the exact same thing again, but the results will be different this time.

Have any of those thoughts tumbled around in your mind? If so, now that you recognize them, dispose of them. Those paradigms only serve to keep you stuck.

Instead, let's consider some constructive thoughts:

- Failure is not a fatal disease, a destination, or a character flaw. It is a learning tool.

- Failure is not a permanent condition, it is a temporary event.

- Failure is an opportunity to stretch and grow.

- Failure is a way to gather feedback.

- Failure gives me the chance to see what doesn't work so I can change my approach.

And finally, let's look at some do's and don'ts concerning failure:

- Don't take the failure personally. YOU are not the failure, it does NOT identify who you are.

- Do suspend emotion from the failure as soon as possible so you can study it objectively to adapt for the next attempt.

- Don't stoop to a victim complex. If you blame everyone else, even if they played a major part in the failure, then you voluntarily give them power over how you think, feel, and act. That's very DIS-empowering.

- Do take responsibility for your part in any failure regardless of how small. However ...

- Don't go on a long guilt trip over your contributions to a failure. Don't wallow in it. Acknowledge it but don't hang on. You can't change the past, so accept it, make amends if possible, and let it go.

- Do focus on what you can learn from the failure and focus your energy on a better future.

- Don't worry about what other people think or say about the failure, and that includes your dream-killer.

- Do shift any negative views of the failure to positive ones. For example, instead of thinking "This failure was horrible. I'll never recover. It means I'm stupid!", shift it to "Okay, so I've learned that wasn't the best way to do it. Now I'm a step closer. I'm also smarter."

See the difference?

In discussing failure, I also want to share my personal view that there are only three ways to fail: 1) not try in the first place, 2) quit, and 3) not learn something from the experience (especially if you blame someone else for the bad results). That's it. Everything else is feedback.

It's okay to fall down as long as you get back up. Even the most graceful dancer or accomplished athlete started with a wobbly little Frankenstein walk. And I guarantee they got some scraped knees along the way. Falling is not failure. Even if something doesn't turn out like you hoped or planned, it was NOT a failure if you learned something from it. So just keep going!

Act Like a Baby

Say what?

No, I'm not referring to crying when you're hungry or screaming when your mom leaves the room.

I'm talking about a baby's genius ability to absorb information and master new skills at a rapid pace. There are no preconceived notions about his ability (or lack thereof) or the timetable for improvement. He just keeps trying until he achieves whatever he wants to accomplish.

Speech for example. A baby coos, then babbles, experimenting with different sounds until the first simple words are formed. Soon they can actually converse with you, their vocabulary increasing daily for the first few years. They can even learn two languages at once, speaking each with the proper pronunciation.

And what about mobility? That new little person laying helplessly in the crib is soon squirming to the corner, then rolling over, and before you know it, he's crawling. He pulls himself up to stand at the side of the couch, cruises around the edges, back and forth, back and forth, until he decides to let go and take that first step.

Pumf! He falls down on his bum. No matter. He pulls himself up and tries again. Pumf! He never stops to think, "This is just too hard. I'll never walk." He doesn't say, "I look so stupid" or "Big sister does it so much better."

No defeat, no judgment, no comparison, no fear. Just focus and determination. He simply keeps trying, over and over, again and again, until at last, he takes a step before falling. Then two, then three. Soon he's dashing around everywhere. A whole new world is open to him.

Was the baby a failure because he fell down? No! What about the 71st time? No!

All the failed attempts were merely practice runs. Feedback. With each effort, his leg muscles got a little stronger, his coordination a bit better, his perception slightly tweaked. The accumulative result was the accomplishment of walking. Then running, skipping, jumping. Then playing hopscotch, riding a bicycle, balancing on a hover board. Compound learning.

It appears that once a child reaches age 4 to 6, this genius learning drastically slows down. Is it a coincidence that at the same time, he becomes aware of other people's judgments and expectations? I don't think so.

He starts noticing other people's adverse reactions and questioning glances. Negative comments reach his ears. Is it possible that his efforts aren't good enough? That HE isn't good enough?

Doubt creeps in, confidence wanes, uncertainty takes its place. The pure joy of learning is dampened. The natural urge to explore and experiment is squelched as he is expected to color within the lines.

Eventually, he conforms to the norm. The genius is stuffed deep inside and his progress dwindles to a fraction of his potential. He joins the herd, forgetting his inborn brilliance.

How terribly sad.

Did that happen to you? It did me. But the good news is, we don't have to stay stuck in the land of the ordinary.

You can choose to rewire your brain to become more like it was in your early years on planet Earth. That's what I meant by "act like a baby." In case you haven't heard of it, it's called brain plasticity or neuroplasticity.

No, that doesn't mean our brains are made of plastic. It means that they can be molded and changed by experience and thought.

Unlike the historical view that our mental abilities were set at an early age and couldn't be changed as we got older, scientists now show that our brains are flexible and adaptive. That is, IF we make choices to expand and stimulate them.

And it doesn't matter what age you are. You can be 19 or 91. Barring effects of serious illness or injury, you can always learn new things to stimulate your mental capacity.

As examples: The actor, Samuel L. Jackson, didn't have a major role until he was 46. Leo Goodwin founded the GEICO insurance company at age 50. Duncan Hines licensed his name for his cake mixes when he was 73. The artist, Grandma Moses, had never picked up a paintbrush until she was 78.

One of my favorites is a personal friend, Sylvia Anthony, whom I met at a Mary Morrissey event in 2016. In her 80s, she had recently published her first book, sharing her life journey, which resulted in over 25 years working with homeless women and children in the Sylvia's Haven shelter. Her passion now is to open Sylvia's Havens in all 50 of the United States. She is an amazing woman who has kept her mind sharp through continual mental stimulation and service.

All those exemplary people made the choice to keep learning and keep trying. You can, too.

Neuroplasticity gives you the ability to exchange a bad habit for a good one. All the positive tips and tools presented in this book can become your new norm.

How?

Direct your attention to whatever new habit you desire. Think about it, picture the results in your mind, think about it some more. Align your actions with your thoughts. When the old pattern tries to resurface, just redirect your attention back to the desired habit. As you repeat this, your brain gets rewired until eventually, the influence of the old paradigm slips into the past.

The New You

It's in your power to advance your passion regardless of what anyone, including your dream-killer, throws at you. That doesn't mean there won't be obstacles. There will be. But instead of letting them stop you, climb over, go around, re-route. Let the overcoming make you stronger, wiser, more compassionate.

Your dream seed will grow into something far greater than you first imagined, if only you open yourself to the possibilities. Please don't limit yourself by thinking small or being so attached to a certain viewpoint that you miss even greater opportunities that are presented. You have everything you need to triumph.

When things don't go your way, toss the blame game out the window. Regroup, think of a different approach, focus on what you have, not what you lack.

Do you underestimate your ability? Stop it! Don't sell yourself short.

Yes, we all have shortcomings, but you can develop a plan to overcome them or delegate tasks in those weaker areas to someone else. Concentrate on your strengths. Take full advantage of them. They will help turn your dream seeds into life-giving gifts to the world.

As you continue to advance as a unipreneur while at the same time nurturing the relationship with your dream-killer, it is quite possible he may one day look at your accomplishments and think (if not say), "Wow. She was right! I'm so proud of her ..."

You will not fail if you CHOOSE to succeed!

ACTION STEPS

For Your Passion:

- Take a good look at the content you are consuming. Are you on overload? If so, prioritize. Pick the program that best aligns with living your passion. Put other content out of sight (temporarily) while you focus on your No. 1 choice.

- Research the word "neuroplasticity" or visit www.Unipreneur.com for more info on how to rewire your brain to learn new things.

- Make a conscious choice to be "complete" on your own without depending on your dream-killer (or anybody else) for validation. You have everything you need within you to successfully live your passion.

- If you haven't done so already, start your own financial accounts for your passion, completely separate from your dream-killer. Remember, you are now a unipreneur. You are succeeding beside him, but not intertwined with him. Whether or not your dream includes big bucks, keep it independent.

For Your Relationships:

- Start a sweetheart journal. Write down your best memories with your dream-killer. The day you met. That weekend at Niagara Falls. The time he tried to make your favorite dinner but set off the fire alarm in the kitchen. Whatever. They can include some of the Action Steps you took from this book.

CONCLUSION

PUTTING IT ALL TOGETHER

*"It's not what you get,
it's what you do with what you get."*

—Omar Periu

Is my history the one I would have chosen? No. But it's moot to say, "If only this would have happened" or "If only he hadn't done that ..." If only, if only, if only. Damaging words that can only keep you stuck.

Do I wish my family would have continued on the path we started together? That is, a church-going, faithful, close-knit group? Absolutely. But the truth is, I'm no longer responsible for my children. They have free agency to choose their own paths. And God knows what they need to progress. After all, they were His children long before they were mine.

Do I wish my house were filled with dream-builders rather than dream-killers? Yes. But then again, I have grown from my experiences. Some of my history may be painful, and I sure wouldn't want to go through it again, but I absolutely love where I am now. I'm grateful for my life. I'm thankful to be me, scars and all.

If you sincerely apply the teachings in this book, you will be grateful for your journey, too. Always reach higher, become more aware, make increasingly enlightened choices, and you can become a unipreneur who makes a positive impact on the world. And you can have a strong relationship with your dream-killer, too. It doesn't have to be one or the other.

Friends

I have two friends that embody opposite sides of the same coin. Both endured horrific pasts and want to move forward. One has discovered and accepted her inner power. The other has not. I continually have a prayer in my heart for each one as they continue to face their challenges.

When Katie (not her real name) was 8 years old, she discovered her father's body after he hanged himself. Her mother died a few years later, and Katie was shuffled among various aunts and uncles, some of which were abusive, leaving her feeling unlovable, worthless, and alone.

How does a child ever recover from something like that? Especially when there is no guidance from a loving adult? Her inner compass was spinning like a pinwheel in a wind storm.

She eventually escaped the cycle by getting married. Thankfully, her husband was not abusive, but she left him after only a few years, mostly because her inner struggles left her unable to accept that she could be in a "normal" relationship.

Katie started her own business, literally throwing all her time and energy into it. I suspect that being busy distracted her from the pain she stuffed inside. She bought a huge (as in HUGE) house even though she lived alone. Well, except for cats and dogs. I believe her pets not only provided desperately needed love in her life, but a sense of self-worth.

Through some bad choices and unscrupulous business associates, Katie's multi-digit business took a dive. Most of her employees were let go as she hung on with only a few clients. Her mansion became not only a financial burden but a "prison," as she called it.

A brief respite came when Katie became a Christian and recognized mistakes of previous years. Making amends where possible, changing some negative habits, and developing a few positive relationships, she started to feel hope. The healing process finally began.

That's about the time I met her through a mutual friend. I liked Katie right away. We had some great discussions on deep topics, and it felt as if we had known each other for a long time. Yet we knew little about each other's history. The past didn't matter, we were friends in the present.

Not long after, tragedy struck again. Our mutual friend was found murdered, apparently shot in her driveway by her husband before he went in the house to shoot himself. It was unbelievable; it was surreal.

Katie slumped into a deep depression. She shared more and more of her difficult past with me. As I listened, it seemed all the bottled-up anguish and fear that had been fermenting since she was 8 years old spewed out unrestrained. But it didn't ease her pain. While she released it verbally, she clutched it her heart.

She sought professional assistance but said neither medication nor counseling helped. After a few years, the despair ravaged her physical health. Severe aches and pains, infections, colds, migraines - she never felt good. It's all she could do to get up in the mornings and run her business with the one or two clients she managed to serve at any given time.

Katie and I don't live close, so we keep in touch through text, social media, and occasionally a phone call. Acting as a sounding board, I think it helped for me to be out of her daily circle so I could look at things more objectively. She also knows that I love her unconditionally.

We hadn't seen each other in person for several months so I recently extended an invitation to dinner. I reached the restaurant first and got a booth so we could talk privately. When Katie arrived, she looked beautiful, as always, but her countenance had changed. Her hug was hollow, her smile strained.

I told her she looked good (truth) but she retorted with, "Everybody else says I look terrible."

For the first time in our friendship, I felt awkward. When she asked how I was doing, I hesitated to answer. Part of me felt guilty for being so happy when, obviously, she was not. I mentally noticed my discomfort.

I finally answered truthfully with, "I'm doing great."

We chitchatted while deciding what to order, but Katie's voice was flat. She exuded negativity. As we waited for the food to be prepared, she brought up her depression and how she was consumed by it. One of her friends had told her she should have more faith in God to heal her and another told her she should volunteer at a homeless shelter so she could recognize all the good things in her life.

Katie was annoyed with those suggestions, saying her friends just didn't get it. She added something like:

"They don't think depression is real, that I can just pull myself up by my bootstraps. But I can't. It's like I'm buried in this deep, dark pit, and there is no way out.

"My dad killed himself. I have a cousin that killed himself. I'm probably going to end up the same way."

I said, "You can overcome it, Katie."

Her eyes flashed with indignation. "I CAN'T overcome it, Laura. It's in my DNA. I can't overcome it."

Great compassion filled me as we locked eyes. She's right. With her belief that she can't overcome depression, she is stuck with it.

She almost had me believing it's hopeless, too. But in my heart, I know Katie's wrong. There is a way she CAN overcome it. If other people can heal themselves of cancer and other diseases through their choice to believe and act accordingly, then so can Katie.

Would it be easy? Definitely not. But it's possible.

As Henry Ford said, "Whether you think you can, or you think you can't - you're right."

Flip-side Friend

I mentioned in Chapter 5 that while focusing on writing this book, I didn't take on any more service projects unless I felt "moved" to do so. There was one project I chose to head that had a big impact on me. I hope it will you, too.

For a Community Day of Service sponsored by our church, the gymnasium was being open for different non-profits to set up workstations. There would be activities such as sewing brightly-colored pillow cases for cancer patients, making surgery dolls for a nearby hospital, and paper-crafting get-well cards for inpatients. Tables would be set up to collect food and clothing for a local refugee resettlement program. The Red Cross Blood-Mobile would be in the parking lot to accept blood donations. It sounded awesome, so I committed to take a break from writing and spend the day helping where needed.

Looking at the flier of organizations represented and lists of supplies needed, I saw an unfamiliar name: Sole Hope. Their only needs were old jeans and sewing scissors. Being a fairly decent seamstress and having taught both my 4-H club members and Girl Scouts how to make tote bags and purses out of blue jeans, I had both.

Not having a clue about Sole Hope, I contacted the person in charge of the event and asked if it mattered if the jeans had holes in them. She responded with something like, "I have no idea. The person representing Sole Hope can't do it now, and I haven't found anyone to take over yet. You're actually top on my list. Would you be interested?"

Even though I had consciously kept my calendar clear so I could laser focus on the manuscript, I immediately knew the answer was "Yes!"

It turns out that part of the Sole Hope mission is to provide handmade denim shoes for children in Uganda after nasty parasites called jiggers are removed from their feet. Thus, the need for old jeans.

I won't go into details about preparation or procedure of my workshop except to say our part in the process was to cut out the pattern pieces for the footwear. These were to be pinned together as kits and sent directly to Uganda to be made into shoes, which are crucial to prevent re-infestation of jiggers.

The Community Day of Service went well although my station didn't have enough sewing scissors to accommodate all the people who were willing to help. I was left with a stack of uncut jeans. My heart was still in the project so I took the materials home with me, setting it near the kitchen table. Perhaps I might be able to cut pieces out during little snippets of time each day while dinner cooked.

My phone dinged with a Facebook invitation to a regional Community Day of Service an hour away. This was a much bigger affair than the local one. I contacted the person in charge and offered to do a Sole Hope workshop. She was very surprised and thrilled to have another non-profit represented.

The regional event not only used their church gymnasium but many, if not all, their classrooms. I shared a large room with another group.

Again, there were not enough sewing scissors for everyone willing to help but many more kits were put together. It was a fruitful morning. It rejuvenated my soul to serve. However, it wasn't until around noon that I realized the biggest reason this particular service project had been put into my heart.

A young, dark-skinned woman quietly slipped into the room and observed for a moment. I stood to greet her. With very good but heavily accented English, she introduced herself as Emman (her real name).

She asked, "What is Sole Hope?"

Turning on a one-minute introductory video downloaded on my laptop, I invited Emman to watch and see for herself. She clapped her hands with excitement as she learned about the project.

"This could help my people!" she repeated several times. "I want to get this into my country!"

I noticed her beautiful smile as she sat across from me to cut jeans. Unlike the rather timid girl who initially stepped into the room, she was bubbling with excitement. She immediately opened up. Her story had great impact on me. I believe it will you, too.

Emman was born in northern Sudan before it split into two countries. Her family follows their homeland's main religion which teaches that women only have two purposes: to serve men and have babies. Women are considered property. Emman has brothers but said her father was so ashamed to have a daughter that he refused to keep her in his home. He sent her to be raised by her grandmother.

I was spellbound as Emman shared some of her experiences. It made me sick to my stomach as she described her treatment on the rare occasions she got to see her parents and brothers. "I was worthless. Worse than worthless. I wondered why my father had even allowed me to live."

Her existence was despairing with no apparent hope of improvement. But it could get worse.

How? My understanding is that Emman was going to be forced into a marriage with a man who also viewed women as property. In essence, she would be his slave to do whatever he desired of her.

Her grandmother fled with Emman to southern Sudan where there were more personal freedoms. Over time, they met a Christian minister, Pastor Tom, who taught that every person, male or female, is valuable in the sight of God. It changed their lives.

Emman was also taught how to read, write, and do basic math - things she was not allowed to do in northern Sudan. She also began to learn English.

Civil unrest in Sudan turned to outright civil war. Unfortunately, during one of the skirmishes, Pastor Tom was killed. Again, Emman and her grandmother fled, this time to Kenya.

During their time in a Kenyan refugee camp, Emman and her grandmother met two Christian missionaries from the United States who baptized them. They also gave her English lessons which Emman said "were much easier to understand than Pastor Tom's method."

Emman flourished in her new-found belief of self-worth. She discovered that she was not stupid as her father told her, but actually very intelligent. She mastered English so well that she was hired as an interpreter by the United Nations.

It's through these connections that she could come legally to the United States and sit across the table from me at the Sole Hope workshop.

I had been so enthralled with her story that I didn't notice my stomach rumbling. A head popped in the doorway saying," Don't forget, there's still plenty of food left."

"Emman, would you like to go to the buffet table with me?" I asked.

Emman shook her head no.

"You aren't hungry?"

"I am very hungry, but I cannot eat in public."

Upon further questioning, she told me that in her homeland, women aren't allowed to eat in public. They must find a private place where no one can see what they're doing. If caught, a woman could be severely punished, even have her hand cut off.

This fear had been so ingrained in Emman that even after two years in the States, she feared to have anyone see her eat.

Knowing Emman's host family, a couple with three daughters, and their strong tradition of eating meals together around the dinner table, I asked, "What about with your host family? Can you eat in front of them?"

Emman smiled sweetly and replied, "Only in the last month have I been able to put something in my mouth while sitting at the dinner table. Just a little bit. And when no one was looking."

Until then, she had been observing their meal traditions without eating. She would take her plate of food to her room afterward to eat in private.

"I have watched Sir Jenson (her name for her host father) interact with his wife and daughters. It amazes me that a man can treat them with such kindness and love. That is what I want in my life. To be loved as a daughter of God."

At that point, I think I heard Emman's stomach growl in unison with mine.

"So, you won't go with me to eat?"

"No. I would rather go hungry."

I looked at a small table with blue jeans stacked on it.

"If I move this little table to the corner of the room and face it where no one can see you, will you eat?"

"Yes!"

I moved the jeans and rearranged the corner.

"Do you want me to bring you food? Or would you like to come with me and choose your own?"

"If you will come with me, I will go."

My heart soared. Together we went to the buffet table where I started with veggies and fruit. For some reason, I expected that's what Emman would get, too. But she stacked her plate high with slices of pepperoni pizza. Her eyes sparkled in anticipation. It was awesome.

I carried her drink back to the room and then returned to the dining area, leaving her to eat alone. My head was spinning with all she had told me.

How blessed I am to be born to parents who value their daughters as much as their sons! I wasn't super close to my dad, but I never doubted he loved me. My life is filled with freedoms that I take for granted.

Upon returning to Emman, I found that she had been doing a lot of thinking as well. Every crumb of pizza had been consumed. As she tossed her empty plate in the garbage, she echoed what I had been pondering.

She said something like, "Since leaving Kenya, I have seen so much waste. There are so many starving people, and yet here, food is thrown out every day. And not just food. So much waste, so much waste. It hurts to see. People here take everything for granted. People have so much, but they cannot see it."

That is the moment I realized why I had met Emman. She had been placed in my life at that moment to jolt me to a new awareness. Becoming a unipreneur has provided me with so much, both tangible and intangible. It's good to want to have expansive lives, but it's also important not to undervalue what we already have.

Just the fact that I'm able to write this book or that you are able to read it, automatically means you and I have great blessings that many do not. The dream seeds placed inside us are gifts from God meant to be nurtured and shared. While conditions may not seem perfect, we can do what we can with whatever we have, wherever we are, and make a positive difference in the world.

But as we move upward, it's vitally important to help others rise, too. Just as Emman now wants to expand Sole Hope into Southern Sudan, your passion, whatever it is, has within it the potential to lift others. I challenge you to become the best YOU. Together, we truly can make a better world.

Final Words

Now you have planted your dream seed in fertile ground, nourished it with a positive attitude and expansive perspective. You have learned about personality styles and love languages, therefore being able to understand your dream-killer enough to present your passion in the most effective way possible. With empowering awareness, you communicated your heart's desire.

You evaluated your dream-killer's reaction or response. He may have continued to stomp on your dream seed. Or he could have given it some serious consideration. You evaluated the interaction and acted accordingly. Regardless of his choices, you realize you are only responsible for YOU.

Your choice is to move forward with your passion, either with your dream-killer's support or without it. Ultimately it doesn't matter. You're committed to develop and share your God-given gifts regardless of obstacles.

You are now a unipreneur who chooses to advance your passion while at the same time strengthening the bond with your dream-killer. Your love for your passion and your love for your dream-killer are not exclusive. You can have them both.

From dream seed to a full-fledged pursuit of living your passion, I wish you all the best. Enjoy the journey. And have an abundant harvest.

CPSIA information can be obtained
at www.ICGtesting.com
Printed in the USA
BVOW06s0604061017
496798BV00001B/1/P